THE
FAKE
NEWS
BIBLE

INTRODUCTION

Fake News Bible is an ambitious title that creates very high expectations and I employed various areas of expertise to meet such expectations.

My starting point was the technical knowledge required to understand the way botnets work and the techniques to make the most out of the Web.

My second point of supply was the techniques and methods related to communication strategies, commonly used by traditional media.

Lastly, I explored the techniques belonging to the field of semantics, psychology and philosophy.

It is my belief that it is only through the careful analysis of the correlation occurring in these areas that the subject of fake news can be dealt with correctly.

Politics and the history of fake news are also an important basis to start from in order to understand the topic. However, this book deliberately focuses more on the relation and the importance of modern techniques, rather than the history of fake news itself, or any subsequent political implications.

Indeed, ample literature already exists concerning the history of fake news.

Information manipulation knows almost no boundaries today and it is obvious that we now live in a "post-truth" world. Cognitive bias have the capacity to upset and twist people's feelings and emotions; they are originating huge media bubbles, which social networks inflate exponentially.

Social networks are now capable of attracting, conditioning and involving an astonishing number of people, at rather accessible costs. They have proven to be indispensable to conduct effective political campaigns, influence financial market trends, or destroy an individual or an institution's reputation.

The first section of the book offers a quick account of famous hoaxes of the past, and an insight into those scientific theories that, were once acclaimed and later disproven by various philosophers and Greek mathematicians over time.

I have also included what I consider a fundamental list of the seven types of disinformation, which will help readers recognise distorted information.

The second part of the book provides a clear description of the procedures and tools used by 'news pollutants'.
My intent was to unfold the 'tricks of the trade' and their peculiar use in news to help people avoid the pitfall.

With reference to the subject of news content, I chose to examine the different types of logical fallacies, which leverage and exploit the hidden errors of human reasoning. I followed a rational order of classification for each fallacy analysed, and I used explanatory and practical examples and cases to demonstrate the principles set out.

The battle against daily disinformation or misinformation must pass through the awareness and understanding of the complex reality behind fake news, where technical, linguistic and mass media oriented elements play a prominent role.

In my opinion, no tool or advice can be effective in battling against disinformation, if both individuals and the community as a whole do not undergo a process of genuine learning and education.

As an example, the purported murder of journalist Arkady Babchenko, staged by the man himself, turned out to be fake, although confirmed by the Ukrainian Government and the Police. A typical case where official sources lacked credibility on an equal footing with the mass.

Mass manipulation can and will only stop if people are supplied with adequate intellectual tools to navigate in a world where information can paradoxically become the worst enemy of democracy.

THE GRAMMAR OF FAKE NEWS

WHAT FAKE NEWS IS

Fake news is the distortion or mystification of news or information, widely distributed with the aim to catch the largest audience possible, specifically for either political or economic reasons.

Fake news initially spreads through sources connected to communication or propaganda agencies and other online newspapers, often characterized by poor journalistic quality.

Occasionally and unimaginatively too, fake news is picked up and redistributed by traditional media channels, such as, television or the printed press.

Spreading fake news via traditional media channels has a much greater impact on people's ability to challenge or question the reliability of such sources of information in a critical fashion. This lack of discernment mainly affects the most vulnerable and intellectually weak sections of population.

It is therefore essential to draw particular attention to the non-accidental nature of fake news. No fake news originates randomly, or it is the work of pure chance.

All fake news refers to a very specific social, political or media situation and, as described further on, it leverages definite logical fallacies with the intent to manipulate moods and feelings of the mass users targeted by fake news generators.

Historian Marc Bloch, in his publication "Memoirs of War", points out that «false news is only seemingly fortuitous", or rather, "all that is fortuitous is the initial incident which triggers off the inherent imagination, although this process can only take place because such imagination has already been sparked under silent buzz».

Marc Bloch

As a socially negative phenomenon, fake news can put democracy at risk to a much wider extent through the passing of incorrect information in the form of satire, entertainment, fiction, or simply as an apparently trivial and unmalicious journalistic blunder.
Initially, we must understand the reason why fake news originates and spreads out, if we want to be able to tell fake news from unintentional mistakes or journalistic inaccuracies.

ORIGIN

The term "fake news" was first entered in the Collins dictionary in 2017 and was later appointed "expression of the year" by the dictionary itself and the Norwegian Press Agency "NTB", thus becoming part of the official jargon terminology.

A series of political and social events have concurred to give strong emphasis to the expression "fake news", although information distortion is as old a history as the world itself.

Hence, the first ten years of the third millennium forced us to tackle an ancient and well-known problem, only dressed with new technologies.
The tendency to manipulate reality for political or economic gain is as intrinsic to human nature as the willingness and the desire to seek the truth.

Totalitarian propaganda

In the previous century, the rise of cruel totalitarian regimes set us face to face with the cynical reality of propaganda, which used information, media and mass culture as a powerful means of control and manipulation.
Soviet, Nazi and fascist press attached great importance to foster the regime version of the truth, taking advantage of many techniques fake news uses nowadays.

The Third Reich contributed with the allocation of yearly funds equal to 1/4 of $1.5bn to the Ministry of the German propaganda, headed by Hitler's right-hand man, Joseph Goebbels. Indeed, it set up a deadly operation-consensus machine.

The Nazi propaganda spread hoaxes and fake news to fuel hatred against the Jews and exalted the myth of the Aryan race.

Joseph Goebbels

A well-known hoax related to anti-Semitism, for instance, narrated that, during the Jewish Easter, some Jewish men had kidnapped a Christian infant to mix his blood with Jewish matzah (unleavened bread[1]).

The Nazi regime even justified the invasion of Poland and fabricated ad-hoc fake news on August 31, 1939 when a group of SS members, disguised as Polish soldiers "attacked" a German radio in Gliwice. Every media picked up and redistributed the news, and the following day Hitler formally announced to invade Poland.

---

[1] https://bit.ly/2sckKJL

The war of the Worlds

In 1938, "Citizen Kane" a most celebrated film directed by Orson Welles, analysed and examined the huge power of information, giving evidence of how easily traditional media could spread fake news, as long as the starting of a totally false fact was introduced by a new media.

Orson Welles during 'The War of the Worlds'

In the same year, Welles also directed a radio series named "The Mercury Theatre on Air" where he broadcast the great classics of literature, such as "Dracula" and "Heart of Darkness". The idea behind the evening program was to transmit "live" news which was very similar to newscasts broadcast by official channels.

"Ladies and gentlemen: we are sorry to interrupt our dance music program, but we have received an emergency news from Intercontinental Radio News.

At 07.40 CET, the bulletin reports that, Professor Farrell from the Mount Jennings Observatory in Chicago, IL, has recorded a series of red-hot gas explosions occurring at regular intervals on planet Mars. Current spectroscopic tests reveal that the hydrogen fuelling explosions is now travelling towards the earth at great speed..."

After this first radio announcement, the program was interrupted a few times and more worrying and alarming news bulletins followed. To give more credibility to the news the program staged a fake interview to an astronomer.

At 20.50 of same day, the New York office also sent out an urgent report saying that a large size blazing object had fallen near a farm in Grovers Mill, New Jersey...claiming ALIENS!

However, "The Mercury Theatre on Air" did not become very popular at the time.

Historian A. Bradley Schwartz[2] reported that, based on an audience lower than one million, only 27% of the roughly 2,000 letters sent to Welles and the Federal Communication Commission, concerned tales of terror and scenes of panic. These cases occurred in spite of the very few thousand people that had been truly deceived by the fiction.

---

[2] https://www.wired.it/play/cultura/2017/09/01/fake-news-orson-wells/

The Boston Daily Globe

BOSTON, MONDAY MORNING, OCTOBER 31, 1938—EIGHTEEN PAGES — TWO CENTS

RADIO PLAY TERRIFIES NATION

The Capital Parade

Lehman Expects Poletti Victory

READY FOR HALLOWEEN

3 FIRES SET IN SO. END HOTEL

22 Guests, Employes Held in Durham as Police Hunt Incendiary

Police, Youth Groups Plan Safer and Saner Halloween

PATROL WAGON, AUTO CRASH

FAIL TO CLAIM

POLICE, BRIDAL Mystery Veils Fatal Injuries

Mars Invasion Thought Real

Hysteria Grips Folk Listening in Late

Many Fear World Coming to End

In real terms the effects of radio drama were much exaggerated primarily by the then American press which published sensational reports and plenty of front pages reading "fake alien invasion orchestrated by Welles" to recount of a terror-stricken America, ready to fight the aliens.

The real gargantuan fake news was propped up by the additional and resulting news following the fuss created by Welles. On the other hand, Welles went along with the game, and later offered his apologies for causing such mass panic, becoming more popular than ever.

Welles' fake story prompted serious thought on the power of new media technologies, namely the radio, which had proved to be able to manipulate the public by spreading false news and information. Welles later stated: "We only wanted to show people not to take pre-packed opinions uncritically and swallow anything they hear on the radio or elsewhere."
The following day, a newspaper published an article entitled "Radio is one of the most dangerous element of

modern culture". If we replace the word "radio" with "internet" we may find similar titles in current news.

The death of Napoleon

The Stock Exchange and financial markets are known to be very sensitive to any contemporary news or event, in reason of their constant pursuit of speculative actions.

A few years ago, a website purporting to be Bloomberg, falsely announced that Twitter was being bought for $31bn, resulting in its stock price soaring, and quickly plummeting.

Already in 1800, the London Stock Exchange had fallen prey to a monumental hoax, which involved various slouch investors. [3]

Napoleon Bonaparte

A man posing as a French officer had travelled to London and introduced himself as Colonel Du Bourg to proclaim the alleged death of Napoleon and the supposed restoration of the Bourbon monarchy.

---

[3]   https://regencyredingote.wordpress.com/2014/06/06/regency-bicentennial-cochranes-trial-for-the-stock-exchange-fraud/

Investors quickly rushed to invest in the London Exchange out of fear of a possible return of the Bourbon monarchy in Paris.

Government bonds surged rapidly on the day, but then around midday, the uncertain climate slowly cooled off the excitement.

In order to reassure investors, the real kicker, arranged at 1pm on a movie-scale, took place when a lavish cart, loaded with men wearing royal uniforms, entered the city and scattered fliers reciting: "Long live the King!", "Long live the Bourbons!".

It was only clear in the afternoon that Napoleon was well alive and many had just been fooled, and duped.

When official representatives unveiled the lie, stock prices, which had previously increased, returned to normality. Only the tiny group who most likely premeditated the fraud made a fortune at the detriment of the many gullible fellows.

The flat Earth

The Earth revolves and it is not flat. Void does not exist. These two statements, deceivingly trivial and obvious, were inadmissible until a few centuries ago. Indeed, over the centuries, scientific progress has gradually removed some of the many misbeliefs that were lingering in the mind of Mankind.

One of the most long-lived hoax in the history of human knowledge is attributable to the great Aristotle.

Aristotle

He supported the non-existence of "void" as opposed to the Atomists, who, like Democritus, asserted that the possible condition of the matter to be "void" existed, that is to say, a total lack of atoms.

The atomism theory did not penetrate the minds insomuch that Aristotle's vision did. He spoke of a finished, complete and full universe. Fifteen hundred years passed before Torricelli, a debunker ahead of his time, could prove the existence of the void in October 1644.

Geocentrism is another false belief that has held men hostage for thousands of years.

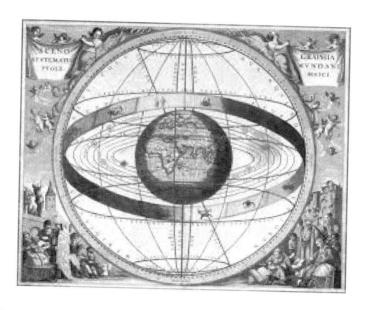

Ptolemaic vision had its roots grounded in Aristotle's writings, where the Earth was at the centre of universe and the Sun or the other planets revolved around it. This theory was accepted, championed and vehemently defended by the Church and the most prominent academic institutions of the time (often connected with the Church), for almost two millenniums.

In order to escape the accusation of heresy, in his preface of the *"De Revolutionibus"*, Copernicus, or whoever wrote it for him, was forced to specify that *the heliocentric scheme* he had described was not a true representation of reality, but merely a mathematical speculative reasoning.

Galileo Galilei

Copernican studies were reviewed by Galileo Galilei, who was obliged by the Pope to renounce and abjure his research and findings, to avoid a conviction for heresy. He escaped execution only thanks to the shelter provided by the House of Medici.

Giordano Bruno, instead, who did not abjure his faith in the Copernican doctrine, was burnt alive.

It was eventually Kepler who confirmed the heliocentric theory, and, a few centuries later, Foucault demonstrated the Earth's rotation around the Sun by carrying out the experiment with the Pendulum device.

Modern physics, Newton's studies and other more recent astronomic studies have now taught us that, the Sun, the solar system and the Milky Way are not standing still either, or rather the entire Universe is continuously expanding, now even accelerating.

The irony of fate is that the current vision of the Universe coincides with the cosmological theory of Giordano Bruno, as detailed in his work "On the Infinite Universe and Worlds" (*De l'Infinito*), published in 1584, which cost him his life.

Despite the scientific community being united on the fact that the Earth is not placed at the centre of the Universe there are still supporters of Geocentrism (and therefore fake-news spreaders). Ample evidence is found on Youtube or Google if one searches "Why the earth is the centre of the universe".[4]

Generally, staunch opponents to already firmly established and important truth, mistrust the bodies and institutions in charge of carrying out scientific research and experiment.

As an example, although the notion of the Earth being spherical has a long-established tradition from Pythagoras to Plato, the false belief that the Earth is flat, still persists.

In his works, Pythagoras himself postulated the sphericity of the Earth, but we found writings of other Pythagoreans who still believed the Earth was flat.

Afterwards, both Plato and Aristotle assumed the Earth was spherical, and even St. Augustine did not deny the possibility that the Earth was a sphere.

As a matter of fact, the first representation of the Earth in the shape of a globe dates back to 1492, however, the sphericity of the Earth was only eventually demonstrated by Ferdinand Magellan who, sponsored by the Spanish Crown, circumnavigated the Earth in 1510.

---

[4] https://www.youtube.com/watch?v=hNutUmthIW0

26

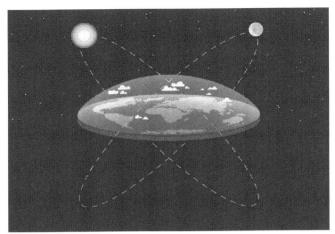

Graphic representation of a flat Earth
and the solar system at the centre

Circumnavigating the Earth, in synergy with the calculations done by Eratosthenes, overturned the conviction of the supposed flat Earth model.

Nonetheless, history is still crawling with supporters of a flat Earth model. They refer to the old and fallacious theories of Diodorus of Tarsus, a bishop and theologian who founded the catechetical school of Antioch, and, among his precepts, upheld "the flat Earth model".

To give an example, the Flat Earth Society[5] is notorious for throwing content to accuse modern science of fabricating fake news with the aim to conceal the actual flatness of the Earth.

According to the Flat Earth Society, the change in climate is also the result of fake news ordered by the lobby of "mightily globalists" to cover up the Earth's flatness.[6]

---

[5] https://theflatearthsociety.org/
[6] https://socialnewsdaily.com/69576/the-earth-is-flat-and-climate-

The Donation of Constantine

Institutions strongly affiliated to Christendom, or others of clearly spiritual nature, such the Church itself, are not exempt either, from producing fake news to conquer power.

We here refer to one blatantly forged document of Christianity which, more than others, conditioned the course of history: "the False Donation of Constantine".

A 13th-century fresco of Sylvester I
and Constantine the Great,
showing the purported Donation
(Santi Quattro Coronati, Rome)

Since the late days of the Roman Empire, the Christian Church, in an effort to justify its temporary authority in the western world had resorted to the "Donation of Constantine" as a ground for its power.

On 30 March 315 B.C., Emperor Constantine the Great supposedly transferred authority on Italy and the western parts of the Roman Empire to the Pope. Besides, the forged document proclaimed Christianity as state religion, thus acknowledging the supremacy of the Church over the Empire.

Twelve hundred years later, in 1517, Lorenzo Valla, an Italian philologist, established the untruthfulness of the document, so strenuously vouched by the Church. It was again a case of news debunking ahead of its time.

Pausanias of Sparta

Earlier on, in ancient Greece, Herodotus narrated of how the concoction of false news had sadly caused the death of Spartan General Pausanias.

Xerxes's concocted plan alleged that Pausanias had plotted the destruction of Sparta. The paper purporting the evidence was a letter where Pausanias had written down his will to betray the city of Sparta. Pausanias was condemned to death although he had strongly denied the charge. He managed to escape execution and fled to find refuge in a sacred temple where he could not be slayed by sword.

Nonetheless, his enemies buried him alive in the temple, where he died of hunger and thirst, nailed by a fraudulent letter that it was very unlikely he had written, as Herodotus and Thucydides reported at the time.

Pausanias (c. 510 - c. 465 BCE)

The ability to manipulate reality through information becomes crucial with the introduction of modern technologies and communication systems known as "many to many". Imagine what Xerxes could do today with a botnet and advertising funds for Facebook if he accomplished to "stitch up" Pausanias with a mundane letter.

DISINFORMATION AND POST-TRUTH

A pivotal expression related to the subject of fake news is the so-called "post-truth", meaning objective data and absolute truth statements are considered of secondary importance.

Oxford University coined the term "Post Truth", and made it "word of the year" in 2016,[7] as published in US magazine "The Nation".

In an article published by Serbian-American playwright Stojan Tesich, it was argued that news on the Iran-

[7]   https://en.oxforddictionaries.com/word-of-the-year/word-of-the-year-2016

Contras affair and the first Gulf War had a lesser impact compared to news on Watergate scandal.

With reference to this subject, Tesich wrote the following: «We, as free people, have freely chosen to live in a sort of post-truth world».[8]

Stojan Tešić

In short, the public perceives and accepts news or generally fake news as true in "post-truth". Fake news is taken on the sole basis that emotions and feelings, previously promoted by different "cognitive bias", are deemed credible in a "theory alternative to reality". Perhaps unsurprisingly too, this acceptance occurs without any tangible analysis of the actual truthfulness or credibility of the stories told. The word 'post-truth' becomes crucial during the first ten years of the third millennium, due to a couple of predominantly-political facts, such as the British referendum to exit the EU, the electoral campaign on Trump and the controversial stands of the President's staff on the climate change.

---

[8] *Flood, Alison (15 November 2016)*

The word 'post-truth' gained prominence again thanks to various publications, namely, ''Geopolitics of emotions'', a work written in 2009 by French political scientist Dominique Moïsi.

The published work suggested that both the web and social networks spread post-truth, and the uncontrolled news flow facilitate the exposure and acceptance/reception of the social media bubble.

The mechanism that produces followers and likes does not debunk falsities. On the contrary, it reinforces them because it tends to polarise similar ideas and opinions, rather than a fair, critical dialogue.

Finally, according to the same political scientist, post-truth in its meaning of political hoax, is transformed into a repeated and endless monologue to replace dialogue between opposing parties.

Current use of the word 'post-truth' is to be attributed to blogger David Roberts, who first used it in a column featuring in the online news website "Grist" in 2010.

David Roberts

In February 2017 Claire Wardle signed an article published in "First Draft News", where he attempted to go beyond the conventional meaning of false or fake news. He tried to define it as the "ecosystem of disinformation", and made a clear distinction between misinformation and disinformation.[9]

In Wardle's opinion, misinformation is the unintentional spreading of false news, whilst disinformation consists in deliberately creating and diffusing false information for commercial or political purposes.

THE VARIOUS TYPES OF FAKE NEWS

As already pointed out, all fake news share the need to pursue a specific purpose through the diffusion of forged information.

We must fully understand the complex working of the information ecosystem by underlining the need for two essential peculiarities:

> 1. Possess an in-depth knowledge of the various types of content and relevant methods to create it

> 2. Comprehend and search for the end purpose, and why fake news spreads

It might be difficult, though, to explain a phenomenon, which manifests itself in ways so diversified and in contexts so diverse. Our book intends to identify and

---

[9] https://firstdraftnews.org/fake-news-complicated/

focus on fake news groups, frequently used to distort online or offline reality.

Moreover, we will define seven methods whereby false content can be shared in the information ecosystem, activating seven types of disinformation:

1. Misleading link: when content differs from title, image and/or caption

2. Misleading context: when part of the content is real, but followed by false contextual information

3. Manipulated content: when image or real information itself are manipulated to mislead reader

4. Misguided content: when information is conveyed to a problem or an individual

5. Deceitful content: if information is passed off as coming from an actual and real source

6. A 100% false content: when entire content is completely false and deliberately intends to deceive

7. Manipulation of satire: when the purpose is not to cause damages, but is satirical and fraudulent

However, it is not sufficient to break down the disinformation process to learn the different types of contents.

We will therefore try to explore the shapes and forms that corrupted information takes, starting from content that is 100% false. We will then examine the content that is manipulated, misconstrued or decontextualized to become mere propaganda, or storytelling propped up by marketing offices.

The various types of fake news and fake content are detailed below.

In the following paragraphs, we mainly refer to content we basically classified as "false".

Hoaxes

Content which is 100% false.
Content which is clearly false and does not have any kind of match with actual reality. It is purposely created to feed a specific strategy of content distribution or propaganda.
Alternatively, it is caused by careless journalistic blunders or false assertions.
Within the context of political propaganda, it is rather common to forge lies and spread them profusely to discredit an opposing party or a political candidate.

During the pro-Brexit campaign, Brexit leaders vigorously maintained that the exit from EU would not result in Britain paying a penny to Brussels.

Subsequently, Prime Minister Theresa May proposed to exit the EU at a cost of £20bn, as opposed to the £60bn demanded by EU executives.

Another popular hoax connected to Brexit during the referendum campaign, was that the United Kingdom's contributions to the EU budget was £350 million a week.

The UK spends more than the amount received by the EU, directly or in subsidized funds assigned from Brussels, although the net contribution paid by the British government is roughly £8.5bn (€11bn) a year, with an average weekly spending of £160m (€200m). [10]

Hoaxes have a natural inclination to sensationalism, which is often necessary to encourage content virality.

---

[10] https://www.tpi.it/2016/06/23/cinque-bufale-sulla-brexit/

They must be able to reach the highest number of readers in the shortest span of time.

In politics, their main purpose is to catch a few extra gullible voters.

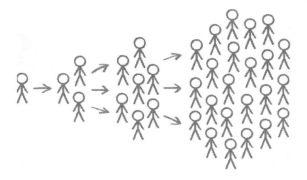

For firms and businesses instead, and specifically in "post editorial[11] world, the primary need is to convey the highest number of users to own digital space and cash in on traffic generated by flaunting Display Advertising.

It is understood, that many news desks go to extreme lengths to draw up and hand out sensational and bombastic news, which is frequently completely false.

As an example, the web often reports false deaths, startling findings or mysterious sights of unlikely animals, or other sensational facts, which are equally unlikely to have happened. This news is handed out by channels suitably chosen in relation to their content virality.

11
http://www.quotidianopiemontese.it/torinovalley/2016/12/18/facebook-pulsante-antibufala-post-verita-post-editoria/

Facebook executives have more than once stated that they will start to encourage programmes to identify hoaxes with ease. They even proposed a "no-hoax key"[12] in 2017.

By so doing, they are implicitly admitting the fundamental role played by social networks in passing out false or misleading content, fraudulently introduced to create propaganda or inflate data traffic in websites.

Zuckerberg's social network attempts have insofar proved unsuccessful in tackling and curbing the spreading of fake content when systems tried to introduce methods "to moderate" fake content.

In addition, as we will see further on, a private company cannot act as guarantor of any form of censorship.

Clickbait

We have so far briefly spoken of how virality plays an essential role in distributing false content.

The correct definition is known as "clickbait" and it entails the introduction of a title intended to entice the viewer with its exaggeratory and extreme character, encouraging other viewers and social medias to click through other websites when captured by these extremely enthralling or apocalyptic headlines.

---

[12]   https://www.lindiceonline.com/osservatorio/cultura-e-societa/facebook-editore-instant-articles/

Clickbait unquestionably implies the ability to reach the highest number of users in the shortest time possible, through that resounding capability which is peculiar to many fake news factors, especially in social media.

From 2008 onwards, "clickbaiting" has ridden the wave of success and gained immense popularity since it became apparent that it assured (and still does) much greater attention on the part of users. Catching attention is a vital aspect for all information channels and newspapers, even the long-established and most authoritative papers.

The press dedicates a great amount of space to articles or multimedia content featuring "clickbait" titles in its online activity.

It is very often a case of clickbait content introduced to inflate online traffic in newspapers to cash in from website traffic generated. It is fair to say, however, that not all clickbait content is necessarily mendacious or reporting false information, since clickbait is indeed a titling method.

We must also point out that there is also highly informative content, which is dressed as "clickbait" with the only intention to appeal more to viewers. (Example:

"The 11 Rulings of the Supreme Court that could revolutionise the United States"), as opposed to news with zero-information content, gaining ground lately despite its trashy or tacky taste. (Example: "We reveal all hot secrets of actress X; click here to find out more").[13]

Conspiracy theories

In early 1900, conspiracy theories based on globalist ideologies were taken seriously in some esoteric social milieus.

Rudolf Steiner's thoughts prevailed with a certain degree of influence among them all. He openly accused the Anglo-American secretive confraternal groups, whose aim was to impose a sort of world economic order to exercise a strong cultural and spiritual predominance on society.

The expression "conspiracy theory" was first used in the United States of America in 1964, with reference to President John Fitzgerald Kennedy's assassination.

---

[13]   http://www.linkiesta.it/it/article/2014/07/29/fenomenologia-del-click-baiting/22388/

The Onion

Friday, November 22, 1963   FINEST NEWS SOURCE IN AMERICA   • • •   Price Seven Cents

KENNEDY SLAIN BY CIA, MAFIA, CASTRO, LBJ, TEAMSTERS, FREEMASONS

President Shot 129 Times from 43 Different Angles

DALLAS, Tex.—President Kennedy was assassinated Friday by operatives of the CIA, the Giancana crime syndicate, Fidel Castro, Vice President Johnson the Freemasons and the Teamsters as he rode through downtown Dallas in a motorcade.

According to eyewitnesses, Kennedy's limousine had just entered Dealey Plaza when the president was struck 129 times in the head, chest, abdomen, arms, legs, hands, feet, back and face by gunfire. The shooting began at 12:30 p.m. and lasted until 12:43 p.m. CST.

In all, 42 suspects have been taken into the custody of the

Parkland Hospital, where doctors with ties to Johnson's inner circle performed a staged autopsy. They pronounced him dead at 2:18 p.m. CST.

The body was then chemically treated by J. Edgar Hoover and put in a decoy casket for transport to Roswell, New Mexico. There space aliens using medical technology beyond the knowledge of man sealed Kennedy's 129 wounds. Kennedy's corpse was then reanimated and rushed to Germany for an emergency meeting with the frozen brain of Adolf Hitler.

After the meeting, Kennedy aides announced plans for the

Namely, the phrase 'conspiracy theory' was used, sceptically and derogatorily, to describe the conclusions reached by the Warren Committee (the official commission appointed to investigate the murder), which had been published in the same year Kennedy died.

The conspiracy theories banged on the door again at the start of the third millennium, when the tragic attack of the twin towers took place on 11 Sept 2001.

According to some bizarre and grotesque theories, the terror attacks had been plotted deftly by US financial markets to let them conduct their ruthless policies in the Middle East, undisturbed.

THE PLANE DOES NOT FIT

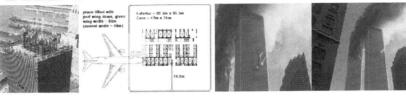

Today, the expression is usually used in a derogatory way to describe any conclusion reached in politics, news or crime, or it refers to phases of the global economy triggered off, and because of a conspiracy plot.

This forced misconstruction generally tends to question facts, or values thoroughly accepted by public opinion, or common sense, and generates a climate of distrust in institutions, the establishment and the intellectual circles.

Fake news flourishes swiftly in intellectually weak minds who struggle to distinguish true from false and struggle to examine the complexity of reality.

Consider the recent case of anti-vaccination movements who typically expose supposed conspiracies, according to which, pharmaceutical companies inject viruses in healthy people to sell vaccines, and consequently, their pharmaceutical drugs.

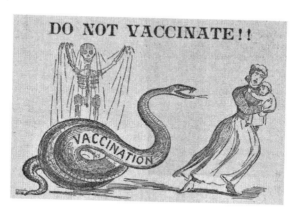

To show how ludicrous and nonsensical their theories are, we stress and outline that, the bulk of those companies manufacturing pharmaceuticals, invest much larger resources in R&D than what they profit in sales of vaccines.

In Italy, the anti-vaccine lobbyists were running rampant to the point that, in 2017, measles cases rose to an alarming 400%[14] due to this sudden and unjustified fear of mandatory vaccinations.

It all started in 1998 when an English doctor, Andrew Wakefield, published an article in a medical-scientific journal. He claimed there was a correlation between MMR vaccines and autism based on a survey conducted

---

14

http://www.repubblica.it/salute/medicina/2018/02/20/news/oms_nel_2017_in_europa_400_casi_di_morbillo-189297053/

on 12 cases. The claim naturally sparked the anti-vaccination movement which keeps growing despite journalist Brian Deer found out the study had been deliberately manipulated and forged by Andrew Wakefield himself.

He was obviously radiated from his profession but the news still floats around and in some countries like Italy, the anti-vaccination movement is on the rise.

Pseudoscience

The term pseudoscience indicates theories, methods and procedures, which do not contemplate any scientific criteria, but pretend instead to be scientific without any cohesion to scientific methodologies - the basis of modern science to prove the validity of a claim with objective evidence.

François Magendie, pioneer of philology [15] was among the first to use the world ''philology while investigating phrenology.

François Magendie in 1822

[15] Magendie, F (1843) Elementary Treatise on Human Physiology. 5th Ed. Tr. John Revere. New York: Harper, p 150. Magendie refers to phrenology as the "pseudoscience of our times"

Pseudoscience became predominant thanks to the works of German doctor, Franz Joseph Gall, in 1800.

He studied and evaluated the morphological specificities of the cranial skull, its lines, depressions and sketches, to identify and determine the mental qualities and personality of the human mind.

All forms of pseudoscience present common aspects that help finding out that some pseudo-scientific theories are actually not scientific at all.

Pseudoscience is often vague, inaccurate and lacking specific measurements, or in some cases, it does not allow measurable results to be considered. Pseudoscience does not acknowledge experimental tests, or it plainly contradicts experimental results. Pseudoscience conclusions often seem difficult to disprove and they are prone to constant changes to escape obvious critical judgement.

Advocates of pseudoscientific arguments also tend to expose the alleged ostracism of the scientific community as stubborn close-mindedness, determined by the pursuit of economic interests, to avail the conspiracy theories.

Different cognitive bias reinforce the notion of these pseudoscientific ideas.

These ideas leverage various bias, such as, the "argument from ignorance", in a rhetorical manner, to state that "if something has not been proved false, it must be true then".

Another cognitive bias, so dear to pseudoscientists, is "the appeal to nature", meaning that everything which comes from nature must inevitably be good or useful.

Among the most-known pseudoscientific theories, we quote homeopathy, which is still deemed incompatible with present biochemical research carried out. Homeopathy supposed therapeutic effects are yet to be proven.

Another example is astrology, which has several million followers all over the world, despite its complete lack of evidence, and what is interesting is that it feed itself on a self-focused publishing market.

Storytelling

In this era of post-narration, people prefer to know about a story rather than a fact.

In the last 20 years, companies largely used narration techniques to give their brand a value it could have not ever acquired otherwise.

Political candidates have also made recourse to storytelling to enhance the pathos of their messages and warm up the hearts and instincts of their voters.

It is proven that our brain is naturally keen on the embrace and acceptance of a story or description, rather than an analysis or a list of objective data (even a correlated-data list).

Various studies indicate that dopamine's release, as a result of an enthralling story and the inducement to immerse oneself in the story and its characters, make storytelling a formidable weapon of communication for a product or brand.

A powerful story is capable of activating various brain areas causing them to interact rapidly so that information is readily usable in our neurological structure.[16] Fake news distribution therefore travels through the use and command of certain storytelling techniques. The fake news messengers do not send stone-cold messages of objective data and axioms, but thrilling stories to stir and make irrationality prevail over objective judgement, of the message first, and the product after.

Shitposting

Shitposting is a technique to steer from the subject of conversation, or it can be a thought-provoking technique and they are both used in the web world.

Shitposting implies massive distribution in the form of comments with irrelevant, teasing, senseless and crass content, to corrupt content quality.

---

[16] https://www.fastcompany.com/3031419/why-our-brains-crave-storytelling-in-marketing

Shitposting was elected "Digital Word of 2017" and it is a technique used in forums long before the arrival of Web 2.0, but it was then considered a form of "Trolling"[17].
It was only in recent times that shitposting became a technique to corrupt rational debate in current social media.

During the 2016 US election, many activists utilised shitposting to diffuse "memes"[18] and published counterfeit images and lewd comments, in order to discredit opponents and competitors.

---

[17] The word **troll** in internet and virtual communities indicates a person who interacts with others through inflammatory, irritating, off-topic or senseless messages to provoke emotional response and disrupt dialogue.

[18] **Meme**: is a cultural symbol or social idea, for example, a trend, fashion, stereotype and verbal expression, a funny gig that is virally transmitted as copy or imitation by propagation, sharing or quotation.

As an example, Palmer Luckey[19], inventor of the 'Oculus Rift[20], set up a group in 2016, with the sole intention to create memes against Hillary Clinton. He was subsequently accused of huge investments in Nimble America, an agency connected to "Alt-Right" - an American company whose main activity happened to be the spreading of "memes" and propaganda content to favour the Republican candidate[21].

---

[19]   https://www.telegraph.co.uk/technology/2017/03/31/oculus-rift-inventor-palmer-luckey-quits-facebook-funding-anti/

[20] Oculus Rift is a virtual reality display worn on the head (English acronym: HMD, head-mounted display). It is considered the best display available in the market today, together with 'HTC Vive.

[21] http://knowyourmeme.com/memes/people/nimble-america

Oculus Rift

One of the most popular (and most shared) 'meme' during the 2016 US elections portrayed a stylised face of Sen. Hillary Clinton captioned by the writing "Too big to Jail" in block capital letters.

Satire and entertainment

It is worthy of mention that not all fake content, or false, corrupted, one-sided, partisan information is originated to pursue a political or economic motive.

Some content is divulged for mere entertainment and in some cases to stimulate thinking.

Satire is no stranger to distorting information or facts either, to supply audience with stereotyped, exaggerated or grotesque images. It often depicts reality in a more complicated fashion than it already is.

In addition to traditional comedians who appear in theatre shows and venues, and that the public can see on cell phones, TV or other devices, the web witnessed the proliferation of flocks of satirically-oriented, digital news. They are dedicated to blatantly false news to ridicule politics or society. The newsmaker always lays its foundations on the virality of the false news, or the title attractiveness.

A unique example of this new type of mock digital news is the Italian website known as "il Lercio".
The mordant authors of "il Lercio" publish humorous and caustic posts in social media, always combined with apparently alarming or derisive headers, which are, in facts, mockery, scorn and outrage against Italy and its politics.

To give you an idea: "China, a new reform of Constitution: Xi Jinping shall continue to be President 10 years after his death", "Trump: "the teacher owning the biggest gun shall be appointed school headmaster" ".

"Il Lercio" focuses on certain topics that go straight to the public's hearts and instincts. The alleged death of a VIP personality, the levy of new taxes and the introduction of laws more favourable to immigrants are only to name a few. In these cases, public opinion reacts instinctively. "We only care about *"Fictional News"*: satire, farcical humour and facetious imagination".

A recent US survey in this regard suggests how satire is not just entertainment, but produces real "political" effects in public opinion.[22]
"Ohio State University" researchers Silvia Knobloch-Westerwick and Simon Lavis have studied the impact of programs that use satire to analyse daily political news and found out that satire and entertainment have a huge power to influence political views.

Silvia Knobloch-Westerwick

The study also outlined that viewers with a low interest in politics prefer to watch satiric programs more than serious political news, or other research programs on politics. Viewers also turned out to be greatly influenced

---

22   https://www.wired.it/attualita/politica/2017/01/24/effetti-satira-politica/

and more malleable by content mystified for entertainment or whimsical purposes

WHY FAKE NEWS IS CREATED

Influence public opinion

In the last ten years, international politics confronted itself with the issue of the ever-growing digital media impact, especially social networks, rather than traditional misleading information and propaganda.

The first electoral campaign that changed the game rules and differed from previous political communication strategies, was Barack Obama's campaign in 2008, during the race for winning his first presidential electoral mandate.

Alec Ross, one of the key players behind the campaign, has often said that, without social networks, it would have been impossible to attain such an historic and important goal, mainly referring to the high rate of voters, in percentage terms, traditionally extremely low in the US until then.

In fact, he stated that it was incredible that through social networks and ''streaming''[23] platforms the campaign had attracted and involved such huge masses of people with relatively accessible costs[24].

---

[23] Streaming in telecommunication identifies any audio or video data flow transferred from source to one or more destinations via

[24]   https://globalriskinsights.com/2016/03/how-social-media-is-changing-political-campaigns/

After the US elections in 2008, Joe Trippi, a well-known political strategist in the Democratic Party, affirmed that, thanks to advertising funds donated by Youtube in favour of Obama's campaign, official videos promoted by Youtube itself were visualized by voters for longer than 14.5 million hours. TV space was bought for a total of 14 million hours. This cost is now estimated to reach at least $47 million.[25]

Besides, we shall bear in mind that, to obtain the greatest efficiency and the highest degree of involvement by voters, social networks allow to "target" and segment the public, also through the content they spread. These features allow specifically tailored and precise content to be designed for every single segment.

---

[25]   https://bits.blogs.nytimes.com/2008/11/07/how-obamas-internet-campaign-changed-politics/

All crucial political events in the first ten years of the third millennium could not help, but tackling propaganda scattered in social networks - a factor that, in the opinion of some experts, has succeeded, at times, to help one side prevail on the other.

Nigel Farage

Online propaganda succeeded in having a heavy impact on US presidential campaigns in 2012 and 2016, Brexit referendum, French elections, the pro-independence referendum in Catalonia and Italian general elections in 2018.

It can be safely assumed that the winning parties were those political forces who, most diligently or cunningly, knew how to use social media channels to participate the different segments of users.

As for Brexit, activists campaigning for "Leave" and the agencies interconnected to the campaign, spread out hoaxes and misleading content with reports of inflated

European budgets, outrageous European taxes and an expected rise in UK salaries in case of exit from EU.[26]

Such false and mystified information generated the online media effect that made BREXIT the most mentioned Facebook word, in the UK, in 2016.

According to analysts, the undecided voters mainly belonging to the British "Working Class"[27] had made the difference, since they changed their minds a few weeks before the polls, influenced by the misguiding themes contained in fake news and propaganda.

Likewise, in the case of the US presidential election in 2016, Donald Trump scored an unexpected success thanks to his extremely simplified communication and the confusing content on sensitive themes, such as, immigration, safety, fighting terrorism and the battle against unemployment.

During his campaign, Trump and his staff lashed out against the figure of Hillary Clinton, on a regular basis, in a sort of "Character Assassination".

There were false, misleading and spurious inquiries on Hillary Clinton's relation with ISIS and Russia. Some worse conspiracy theories like the "Pizzagate" reported that children were harboured in the basement of a famous pizza place in Washington DC, to be allegedly raped by a group of powerful people. Hillary Clinton and

---

[26] https://www.theguardian.com/commentisfree/2016/jun/20/brexit-fake-revolt-eu-working-class-culture-hijacked-help-elite
[27] Working class

John Podesta (Campaign Manager of Hillary Clinton [28]) were supposed to have taken part.

The news was obviously false and totally unfounded. Fact-checkers quickly disproved the allegations a few days after the news broke out[29].

Despite its falsehood, the "Pizzagate" scandal stayed a hot trend in social media for many weeks and provoked great media turmoil.

The fake content was picked up by thousand people and spread everywhere. Even Trump's Security Advisor, General Mike Flynn reported the news. The allegation gathered such momentum and visibility to egg on a young man, Edgar Welch, aged 28, from North Carolina, to visit the pizza place and threaten the staff with a rifle

---

28   https://www.independent.co.uk/life-style/gadgets-and-tech/news/pizzagate-what-is-it-explained-hillary-clinton-paedophile-conspiracy-gunman-fake-news-a7456681.html

29 https://www.snopes.com/fact-check/pizzagate-conspiracy/

gun, one evening in December. Welch was tried and sent to jail for four years in June 2017.

Similarly, the fake news campaign rewarded Italian political parties and populist movements, such as, the League and the Five Stars.[30]
All across 2017, fake news sent out misleading content pertaining to vaccines, safety, immigration, stability, international agreements and exit from the EU.
Fake news learnt how to catch voters from the anti-establishment and populist forces whose total votes (Five Stars plus League) accounted for 50% of overall electorate.

Fake newsmakers scattered the web with news on alleged family nepotism or cronyism perpetrated by the Democratic Party, or messages containing pseudo-racist information on particular benefits allegedly granted to immigrants by institutions[31]. This propaganda mostly favoured the messages from the League Party and the 5 Stars.

Hence, the close tie between the actions and doings of a political party in social channels and the party's outcome at elections is undeniable.

What emerges is that the role played by propaganda content, fake news and "shitposting" against political

---

[30]   https://www.nytimes.com/2018/03/01/world/europe/fake-news-italy-election-europe.html
[31] http://espresso.repubblica.it/inchieste/2018/01/03/news/migranti-e-salute-basta-bufale-ecco-tutto-quello-che-bisogna-sapere-1.316458

candidates gave a leg up to seize votes from habitual non-voters, or those traditionally undecided. A fact that clearly did not happen to traditional parties.

More importantly, the web and social networks have demonstrated how fundamental their role was in the last ten years when, in March 2018, the firm "Cambridge Analytica", came under fire, together with some politicians and advisors connected with the populist right-wing party, like Donald Trump, Farage or Steve Bannon, an advisor of Trump and co-founder of CA.

A "repented" pundit (i.e. whistleblower) by the name of Christopher Wylie, unveiled to the press that CA had invested approximately $1m, in 2015, to collect data from million Facebook users, breaching its terms, rules and conditions of use in many instances.

Christopher Wylie

All data collected was allegedly ordered by target

segment, to facilitate social network propaganda against political candidates.

The press largely blamed Facebook - Mark Zuckerberg's platform, and condemned the social network irresponsible conduct in the treatment of user personal data. Ultimately, FB was used as a scapegoat.

In any case, we must remind us that Facebook is not the only platform where you can retrieve user data and profiles.

There are many tools to carry out "Data Parsing"[32] from other social networks like Twitter, Linkedin, Pinterest, Youtube, Reddit and even Google.

Influence markets and decision-makers

A wise and prudent distribution of fake news can influence financial market trends since their activity is based on analyses resulting from data and information, which, in some cases, turns out to be inaccurate.

The stock market can suffer a sudden crash because of fake news, as it happened in 2013, when a "Tweet" from Associated Press reported of an explosion where Obama had been injured.

---

[32] https://wp.nyu.edu/smapp/data-collection-and-analysis-tools/

The AP (Associated Press) later offered its apologies claiming its account[33] had been hacked[34] and, although the accident had never taken place, the US stock exchange burnt out $130bn worth of stocks[35] in a few hours. Markets returned to normal in 24 hours once that fake news was debunked across the world.

Therefore, imagine the economic advantage from knowingly manipulating the price of stock and shares, even just for a couple of hours.

The capacity to juggle the ups and downs of stock price because you control the falsehood or veracity of information. Then, the power to decide to debunk the

---

[33] An account is the complex of operations, tools and content attributed to a user name in specific operational environments, not only websites, or for use in internet services, to access most software applications.

[34] A skilled person who is an expert on programs, systems and information security, having the capacity to enter computer networks without authorisation or capable of developing computer viruses.

[35] https://www.telegraph.co.uk/finance/markets/10013768/Bogus-AP-tweet-about-explosion-at-the-White-House-wipes-billions-off-US-markets.html

news gives you an important edge over markets and capitalise on the interests yielded by stock price oscillation.

Equally, fake news can influence vast groups of public opinion as consumers, but also key "decision-makers" in private industry, businesses, civil or government sectors where executives make important decisions.

As an example, a leading company could recruit a communication agency to carry out activities aiming at influencing politicians to urge legislation favourable to the company industry in question. Sometimes, news is purposely generated in favour or against a specific industry under the claim that such news is connected to employment, or environment or the citizen's welfare. Then, mechanisms to activate fake or real users are implemented to report online content, which is supported by number of likes, shares and comments, to reach target person or company. This procedure proves to be highly effective since it leverages vulnerabilities of human perception. This methodology is amply described in the chapter dealing with the numerous techniques adopted to confuse argument and they are accompanied by relevant examples.

Fake news on weather forecast, such as, catastrophic droughts, extremely cold winters or other natural calamities, may exert influence on energy stock strategies for companies operating in energy production or sale.

Fake news on fuel price rise, (or fake news indirectly causing a rise of fuel price), such as, a news network rumouring an alleged war between the Emirates and the USA, will determine a change in the strategy prices of products closely linked to fuel.

Fake news on food harmfulness and the alleged unethical production of palm oil played a major role in the decisions made by executives of the food industry. Executives even changed recipes of some products, or explicitly labelled product package as containing 'no palm oil', a nutrient suddenly infamous for public opinion.

Gluten experienced the same bad luck and it has now become number one enemy of food fashionistas...

Clamour over harmful ingredients used in food industry also hit some Italian and international brands like Barilla and Ferrero. The latter stood up for its most notable product, Nutella, culprit of excessive palm oil, whilst other competitors rapidly surrendered to fake news that affected their products.

Those two Italian brands set themselves apart from the rest with a strong communication campaign aimed at debunking that fake news[36] and protected product's original recipe. They struck a remarkable success in terms of growing online brand reputation and increased their trust relation with customers.

Broadly speaking, the possibility to manipulate the public's attention to the point of exerting influence on a "decision-maker" does not occur exclusively in B2C

---

[36]   https://www.barillacfn.com/en/magazine/food-and-society/fake-news-is-contagious/

69

relations (Business to Consumer), but also in B2B relations (Business to Business) if affected by this type of information   manipulation.

Imagine the case of a company supplying technical materials to other companies.

A potential competitor, attempting to enter a specific market, does not find any available space because of main player's solid expansion in the industry. He/she decides to start spreading fake news to damage the leader's reputation and undermine the market niches resulting from the distrust created around main player and left out by those gullible suppliers falling prey to the fake news.

Monetise traffic

In December 2015, the New York Times published a report stating that digital advertising expenditure would grow by 13.5% the following year. It was expected that, by the end of 2017, online digital advertising volumes would exceed television space acquired in the same period[37].

Already in early 2000, online advertising had allowed companies through what is known as "Display Advertising"[38] to propose ad content and chose websites on the basis of target markets.

---

[37]   https://www.nytimes.com/2015/12/07/business/media/digital-ad-spending-expected-to-soon-surpass-tv.html

However, the arrival of web 2.0 caused a major uproar in the world of online advertising through social networks. New content flows were created for users to interact in very diverse ways.

In 2008 when Facebook snatched Sheryl Sandberg from the ranks of Google[39], it entrusted the executive with one major objective: sales turnover.

Sandberg went well beyond her function and control at Google and used the bulk of user data to set up segments to sell through the purchase of sponsorship in FB platforms.

Companies were now able to extract data on the basis of campaigns purchased in social networks and could conceive custom-made "funnels" according to the segments the advertising campaigns focused on.

New forms of storytelling and ways to promote own brand started; marketing content had now been knocked over

---

[38] Display advertising uses the pay-in space within the user's interest content where to sponsor product/service.
[39]   https://www.nytimes.com/2008/03/04/technology/04cnd-facebook.html

with the use of images, videos and text content in devices and screens.

Big brand advertising is now designed not only to be seen from mobile, but also tends to follow and adapt to the same virality patterns of other entertainment or propaganda content. This new scenario is forcing companies to seek increasingly engaging content and exploit data and profiles extracted from previous campaigns.

It is likely that, in some cases, the use of fake news and mystified content within a strategy frame, may give an added value to the company, or wreak damage to the competitor's reputation, pretty much in the same way we discussed for propaganda.

Think of all the hoaxes circulating and regarding the catering industry. Take McDonalds,[40] for instance, who had to officially deny the various claims circulating to tarnish the image of its products more than once.

To quote yet another emblematic case pertaining to the food industry, and which occurred in the past few years, we shall mention the many brands which exploitatively labelled own product using the "gluten-free", "no palm oil", "fat-free"[41] tag to sponsor product according to the momentary trends, often relying on some authentic fake news.

---

[40] http://www.hoax-slayer.com/mcdonalds-coffee-contains-french-fry-grease-hoax.shtml

[41] http://www.insightsnow.com/misinformation-hurting-food-business/

In 2017 palm oil suffered a large-scale and massive media attack based on the alleged claim of its harmfulness ', without any proven scientific basis.

For fear of plummeting sales, marketing executives launched new lines of products, free from palm oil and, where such an ingredient was not part of the recipe, decided to add and specify the product tag 'free from palm oil'.

Palm oil was rehabilitated by the scientific community in the same year[42], however, the media wave did not slow down at all, and we still see product labelled ''palm oil free' in supermarkets.

Unfortunately, marketing is not the only victim of fake news. Consider the repercussions that a wrong weather forecast might have on company strategies, whether that information is unintentionally wrong or actual fake news.

False weather forecast could compromise the choice of investments for a farm.

---

[42]   http://www.oliodipalmasostenibile.it/coldiretti-e-la-posizione-sullolio-di-palma-fact-checking-vs-fake-news/

In view of a chilly winter, the energy industry could increase the price of energy stock reserves.

The same in general can be said for energy suppliers of many resources and raw materials of all kinds.

Logistics plans its business activity based on season forecast; long-haul shipping, for instance, takes into account weather forecast to pick up best routes, especially at sea, where unfavourable weather conditions take their toll.

The financial trading of commodities, such as coal, oil and sources of electric energy is also affected by direct or indirect news regarding any changes in raw material prices.

Finally, the most explicit and noticeable source of revenue for fake news publishers is monetise from traffic generated through advertising in the web.

By the same token, the publishing aspect of fake news shall not be overlooked.

Paul Horner,[43] the late writer, known for having set up one of the most popular fake news websites, once declared he could earn more than $10,000 a month from Google Ads profits, raised from fake news websites. He added that some clickbait content could sometimes return $9,000 a month if extremely viral.

---

[43] https://www.theguardian.com/us-news/2017/sep/27/paul-horner-dead-fake-news-trump

Paul Horner

Other ways to make profits from fake news are connected with the unauthorised and improper use of a known name to sell a product. Among the most exploited names, we shall mention Elon Musk - used profusely in articles announcing his exit from business and his creation of a new cryptocurrency.

This is obviously a humbug against users who are likely to purchase a fraudulent product, and it is also a fraud against Elon Musk.

Nonetheless, this type of fake news should be stopped and reported immediately. Elon Musk should press charges against unknown persons although the law and traditional procedures move much slower than fraudsters who change identities and disappear in no time at all.

A typical humbug using Elon Musk name

Character assassination

A man's reputation has always been its most important asset.

Since ancient Roman times, enemies were fought by sword, and with use of pen and paper too.

The "Damnatio memoriae" was a Latin phrase to literally signify a person must not be remembered (condemnation of memory).

In Roman law, the phrase indicated a punishment passed by Senate to erase any trace of an individual from history, as if he or she had never been born.

It was a very harsh sanction applied to traitors and those who brought discredit to the Roman state, enemies of Rome and the Senate.

For obvious reasons pertaining to costs versus benefits, the condemnation of memory was exercised by those in power against enemies (those who had fallen from the grace of political power).

This has influenced and altered views and opinions of the Roman chronicle, which we now know as historiography, known to be written by winners.

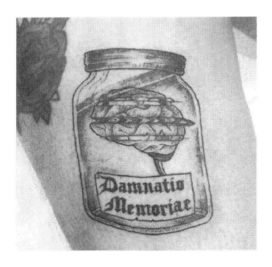

The art of rhetoric has evolved with the passing of time, encompassing some aspects of the "Damnatio

77

Memoriae" and conveying those aspects onto the need to discredit an individual before his final demise from power. Discredit an opponent has therefore acquired an increasingly important significance with the advancing of social media in society.

Introducing different media, such as, the press or television, along with the radio or web, gave rise to the techniques of "Character Assassination".

The systematic destruction of someone's reputation is a long-lasting and intentional process aiming at ruining a person, institution, social group or nation's credibility.

The "International Society for the Study of Character Assassination" specialises in academic studies and research on the destruction of reputation, occurred in past, modern, and contemporary history.

Attacks to reputation can be divided into three different types.

Attacks among peers or people of same standing, which can be the case of some democratic elections.

Attacks called "Top-Down", in cases perpetrated by authoritarian regimes, which decide to destroy a dissident's reputation.

An historic case in point is Martin Luther, condemned and vilified by the Catholic Church following the Protestant Reform, or still the case of "Gao-Rao" in communist China[44].

---

[44] https://link.springer.com/chapter/10.1057/9781137344168_13

Martin Luther

The third type of "Character Assassination" is Bottom-Up" attacks, typical of riots against authoritarian regimes.

History counts famous cases, such as, the insurrection against the Duke of Alba during the Dutch revolution, or the destruction of Hitler and Mussolini figures during the European   resistance.

Recent media now offers new different channels to spread content apt to destroy an opponent's reputation. They enable the process of "Character Assassination" to reach a very high number of people in very little time, and manage to establish the viewer's level of involvement and the content's degree of penetration that ruins the reputation   of   our   target.

We assume we want to weaken a political opponent, or leak a piece of news to tarnish the reliability of a newly appointed CEO, or slander a journalist's name, or a group of experts to invalidate an awkward scientific thesis or analysis.

Our first and foremost move is to collect information, either true, false, or distorted and manipulated, to damage the image of our target and undermine its credibility.

Secondly, information must be sent out trying to reach the highest number of users. Whenever possible we shall try to reach users falling into the group of people emotionally prone to involvement with hoaxes or trickery or fallacious content, due to their prior prejudice and existing   beliefs.

The world of politics thrives with cases of "Character Assassination".

We can quote two recent political events, which were influenced by this process.

The 2016 presidential elections, amply conditioned by "Character Assassination" against Hillary Clinton[45], accused of many different wrongdoings diffused by a network of fake news and shared by thousands of users despite the work of fact-checkers and the news being debunked quickly.

---

[45]   http://www.debate.org/opinions/is-hilary-clinton-undergoing-a-character-assassination

The impeachment of Dilma Rousseff, accused to have been part of the Petrobras scandal with other managers of the Democratic Labour Party and her alleged involvement in other unlawful acts.[46]

Dilma Rousseff

---

[46] http://www.bbc.com/news/world-latin-america-43554395

THE DIGITAL CONTEXT

Social media

With the arrival of the Web 2.0, in 2007, the year when social networks started to become widespread worldwide, content distribution underwent a democratization never seen before.

Anyone could open an account in social media and potentially reach million people with a message.

This mechanism of User Generated Content accomplished an evident revolution in traditional media too, compared to previous "Many to Many" information.

In early 2010 all traditional media already distributed large sections of their content via social media platforms, experimenting new ways to establish contact with readers, listeners or fans.

Social network mechanisms work on the possibility that users can interact with content created in turn by other users, and originate feed (i.e. custom lists), which ensure this content flow can be visualized.

In all social networks, the algorithm that regulates the score during the interaction of different content is the same as the algorithm which allows content to have a better distribution in a social platform.

Facebook, the most widespread social network in America now accounts for more than 2 billion and a half users, and it is the largest community in the world.

Facebook algorithms have undergone many changes over the years to fight fake and hate content.

Initially, algorithms only favoured the distribution and visualization of content which users interacted with most, such as likes, comments, shares ("Retweets" in the case of Twitter or "shares" for LinkedIn),

Later in the years, Facebook algorithms refined content distribution on the basis of other factors, with the dual purpose to customise the experience of users and advertisers alike.

The selection mechanism Facebook algorithms use to custom-make user experience, frequently determines that users surf across a "Filter Bubble" which, for its very nature, tends to polarise tastes, beliefs and opinions.

The arbitrary choice to connect with certain "friends' or follow specific "pages" constitutes a key factor in determining which sources "feed' content comes from, providing cognitive bias of different types in many cases.

Within these user-specific feeds, users find content with a higher degree of involvement. This amplifies even more the capacity to reach more feeds connected with further users who have already interacted with that specific content.
"Virality" is an entrenched and essential feature of the world of hoaxes, humbugs and fake news content.

A survey on fake news, conducted by the "Massachusetts Institute of Technology" which we have previously mentioned, analysed how fake content has a much better capacity of reaching a higher number of readers, compared to more balanced or more sensible content.

Although we have already mentioned that fake news to manipulate politics or the economy has existed since the dawn of time, new media have made it very cost-effective, and, in some cases, maximising the potential distribution of fake news content.
Throughout the whole 20th century, a company was required to invest thousand dollars to purchase advertising space in newspapers, and spend millions for TV commercials.
Politics was at times able to finance entire newspapers, radios and TV channels to ensure adequate coverage of

its propaganda content through those traditional media channels.

Nowadays, anyone can set up a website with the layout of a webzine, or online news, with relatively modest resources. Its content can be sent out via social platforms to potentially reach many hundreds million people with a single post.

The hyper-accessible and massive distribution of content has produced great fuss in the most popular social networks, such as, Facebook or Twitter.

Since early 2000, fake news websites dedicated to satirical and deceptive content have increased at an exponential rate. During major political events or particularly hot topics of current news, fake content reached alarming levels according to observers and commissioners alike.

Propaganda agencies were often responsible for some manipulative influence exercised during some politically important events recorded between 2015 and 2017. Namely, the US presidential election above all, or the Russian polls, the Brexit referendum, Italian and French general elections.

In 2018, following the statement of a former developer at Cambridge Analytica, a firm mostly concerned with data analysis, the Datagate scandal broke out and former Trump's Advisor was proved to have strong connections with the company. Steve Bannon was accused to have collected more than 200 million profiles with the aim to better target his propaganda content during the presidential campaign.

Steve Bannon

The practice of voter profiling is certainly not new at all during electoral campaigns, or in marketing in general. The unprecedented novelty was the capacity to collect a huge amount of data from an equally huge container of personal profiles. Users themselves, like in Facebook's case, made those accessible.

Despite Facebook's previous steps to change some of his terms and conditions to avoid the unlawful retrieving of personal data, Cambridge Analytica managed to breach the access to retrieve thousand data without permission.

To make matters worse, Facebook decided not to report the intrusion of the application CA had developed to collect data, that is, YouDigitalLife.[47]

---

[47] https://my-digitallife.att.com

The oversight cost Zuckerberg, CEO of Facebook, the blue social network, a five-hour Congress auditioning, where Senators and Congressmen expressed serious doubts over the platform's effectiveness in the management systems used to notify users that their data was being collected by advertisers. A few US Senators pointed out at some crucial shortages in the social platform business model, and the encrypted systems, which Facebook and other web services use to protect user content and Privacy.

Cambridge Analytica case sparked a series of fake news pointing fingers at the role Facebook played in selling data to presumed "Data Brokers[48].

Facebook did not specifically sell user data, but it cashed in from the procedure that allowed advertisers to access profiled users automatically. Automatic access happened through tracking down all actions Facebook users do (likes, comments, shares, interests and personal information entered when registering).

For all its drawbacks though, the Cambridge Analytica affair had the merit of shedding further light onto a problem, which is at least five years old.

48

43   http://money.cnn.com/2018/04/11/technology/facebook-questions-data-privacy/index.html

Advertising in fake news

Advertisers are Facebook real customers, although social platform users are, of course, an integral part of Facebook Community.

Among advertisers, we must count those who publish informative editorial content, either real or newsworthy, be it fake, mystified, satiric or entertaining.

Ad, which is short for advert, is any commercial space purchased in digital contexts. Advertising content may be spread out via two different streams: inside a social circuit, such as, posts or sponsored ads, published in Facebook, Instagram, LinkedIn or Twitter; or else by using content sponsored in webzine articles and posts.

It can also be spread in online newspapers which sell available commercial spaces to their advertising networks.

Costs of commercial space in partner advertiser websites depends much on the traffic volume generated in websites sponsoring the content; or it can be based on the advertiser's ability to adopt a policy of strict "targeting" within the classification of advertising posts.

The average cost to reach a Facebook user is roughly half a dollar per user at this book's time of printing. [49]

Fake or deceptive news passed through *AD*, allows advertisers to focus on an extremely specific segment of public, therefore, maximising the efficiency of fallacious content.

In 2017, Larry Kim, US social media expert, took on an experiment to correlate *AD* published in social media and fake news spreading.

Larry put in place a fake website, similar to CNN's, and opened up a Facebook page identifiable with a logo very much like CNN logo.

He wrote fake content headers such as "Anti-Trump Activist admits: I was paid $3,500 dollars to stage a protest against the president" and later shared his newly created Facebook page. Then he published an *AD* fully dedicated to the post itself and picked up an audience from a geographic area consistent with fake news

---

[49] https://aggregateblog.com/facebook-ads-cost-and-bidding/

content. Larry used the "targeting" technique and decided to diffuse fake news to all users that had already interacted with posts related to US conservative policies.[50] Larry succeeded in spreading his fake news to more than 4,500 people and received more than 100 interactions to his post, with a tiny budget of $50 dollars.

Interactions to posts generally originate what is called "snowball" effect - enabling a higher number of people, dependent on how many comment, like, or share and advise to read post.

The more interactions an advert gets, the higher the number of users reached in a systematic order - which will lower the average cost to reach user. For example, the cost of user interaction afforded by Larry Kim during his experiment was close to $0.20 dollars.

Another way to spread *AD* containing posts, blogs or fake articles, is a technique to manipulate results deriving from search   engines.

The main search engines like Bing, Yahoo or Google allow advertisers to purchase premium space based on specific "keywords" selected during search.

These techniques fall into the SEM category (Search Engine Marketing) and allow advertisers to take part to automatic micro auctions where they can secure the very first result among those sponsored by search engines, based on "Keywords" consistent with sponsored content.

Search engines also offer very different targeting options, from choice of age group, sex gender to geolocalization.

---

[50]   https://medium.com/marketing-and-entrepreneurship/facebook-ads-fake-news-and-the-shockingly-low-cost-of-influencing-an-election-data-ca7a086fa01c

It is not uncommon that companies specialising in SEM techniques also act as distributors of fake content[51].

SEO (Search Engine Optimization) is also a technique to promote content which does not entail direct money investment in advertising channels.

Strictly speaking, SEO is not an actual AD since it does not invest money directly in advertising channels. However, we mention it because it is a possible and important tool to use within the area of fake news spreading.

SEO (Search Engine Optimization) is a technique of web writing, which allows a given content to appear more suitable to the "eyes" of spider algorithms used by Google and other search engines. This applies to content

51   https://searchengineland.com/meet-fake-news-online-marketing-world-google-loves-review-sites-279589

dealing with similar topics and most specifically a specific search keyword.

The dark side of SEO[52] also includes the possibility to design a customised editorial process to obtain systematic results when fake and mystified content is placed. Fake content will bear relation to a precise keyword, also consistent with your communication strategy and propaganda.

Bots

Internet bots (an abbreviation of robots in information technology) are software applications accessing network and using same channels as human users do.

Bots are programs that automatically access pages for index-linking (spider), bots can be the non-playing characters of video games, or programs which automatically send messages in chats, and so on.

---

[52] https://www.theguardian.com/technology/2016/dec/04/google-democracy-truth-internet-search-facebook

Basically, bots are programs performing task automation, which would otherwise be too complex, repetitive or onerous for humans.

In the last few years, with the arrival of social media and the traffic monetized from websites, bots started to be strongly debated, especially those intended to look and behave like humans and able to surf and interact with web content.
Social bots can perform the most varied tasks concerning commercial strategies or the spreading of propaganda.
By and large, the use of bots is fairly common by agencies selling fake followers, or false visualizations and interactions.

Automated programs allow these companies to artificially create thousands if not millions of profiles, directing them to a predetermined URL, which aims at targeting a specific post, multimedia content or profile.
In telecommunication and information technology, the phrase **Uniform Resource Locator (URL)** indicates a sequence of characters which unequivocally identifies the address of an Internet resource, typically on a Host Server, made accessible to a Client.

Robots crowd Twitter brand profiles: study

Ilaria Polleschi

2 MIN READ

MILAN (Reuters) - Up to 46 percent of Twitter followers of companies with active profiles could be generated by robots, or bots, a study by Marco Camisani Calzolari, a corporate communication and digital languages professor in Milan, showed on Friday.

The academic analyzed feeds of 39 international and Italian brands, including @DellOutlet, @BlackBerry, @CocaCola, @IKEAITALIA and @VodafoneIT, trying to distinguish fake followers from real ones based on their behavior.

"The number of followers is no longer a valid indicator of the popularity of a Twitter user, and can no longer by analyzed separately from qualitative information," Calzolari said.

*Reuters - Article about Twitter Fake Followers
and Bot research by Marco Camisani Calzolari*

In 2012, I was the first to publicly raise the issue of "fake followers". I practically demonstrated how an algorithm could generate conspicuous shares of followers and how some followers of multinationals, politicians and celebrities were fake.

The share of followers was generated by a network of ad-hoc bots, purposely created or routed to inflate the number of followers in social media pages and profiles.

Fake followers are normally inactive profiles, artificially created by algorithms, which take information from the web and pour it into fresh, newly forged profiles.

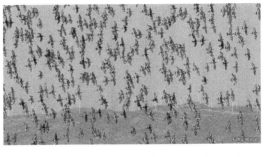

*The Economist - Article about Twitter Fake Followers and Bot research **by Marco Camisani Calzolari***

My study was subsequently picked up and quoted by international magazines and gave rise to a sequel of activities peculiar to "Social Media verification", which are still continuing today.

In 2017, the agency "Marketing Mediakix" [53] conducted an experiment which proved how some semi-professional or would-be bloggers, deliberately falsified their own "Vanity Metrics" (number of followers and interactions) as a shortcut to reach (accomplished) blogger status with the aim of getting paid more money by big brands to sponsor their products.

The survey firstly showed how easy it is to get thousands of real users involved, once you conquer a few thousand false followers, and secondly, the study outlined how inexpensive the services offered by agencies who sell followers, are.

The average cost being $8 dollars for around 1,000 false followers.

Already largely used in show business or by media people, "social" bots are gaining more of a political ground. An increasing number of candidates now use services provided by "digital PR" agencies to turn their propaganda into more powerful and riveting messages.

---

53 https://www.independent.co.uk/life-style/gadgets-and-tech/social-media-experiment-fake-instagram-Accounts-make-money-influencer-star-blogger-mediakix-a7887836.html

News | Opinion | Sport | Culture | Lifestyle

World ▶ Europe US Americas Asia Australia Middle East Africa Inequality More

Hot or bot? Italian professor casts doubt on politician's Twitter popularity

Comedian turned politician Beppe Grillo says academic is wrong to suggest more than half of his online followers are fake

Andrea Vogt *in Milan*
Sun 22 Jul 2012 17.59 BST

f 🐦 ✉ •••

🔵 This article is 5 years old

An Italian professor has found himself at loggerheads with his country's rising political star Beppe Grillo, after claiming that more than half of the comedian turned politician's online followers are fake.

Marco Camisani Calzolari, a Milanese professor who divides his time between Milan, where he is a professor of corporate communications at the IULM university, and the UK, where he founded several web start-ups, developed an algorithm he believes can distinguish human users from fake robot ones, known as "bots". In June, he used his mathematical method to analyse 39 international and Italian brands, including @DellOutlet, @BlackBerry, @CocaCola, @IKEAITALIA. He found a high percentage of their followers were fake.

*The Guardian - Article about Twitter Fake Followers
and Bot research by **Marco Camisani Calzolari***

In 2012, my study on followers involved major Italian and international brands like Vodafone, Ikea, Coca-Cola and others, as well as some prominent Italian politicians.

For instance, my survey remarked that more than 50% of Beppe Grillo's partisans were false followers[54]. Essentially, my research only wanted to highlight the

---

[54]   https://www.theguardian.com/world/2012/jul/22/bot-italian-politician-twitter-grillo

99

ever-growing importance of bots in political communication.

My study was rather successful and stirred some fuss at the time, although today the notion that political candidate profiles have a huge number of fake followers is widely accepted. Politicians have acknowledged the need to have a bot network to give each propaganda message a strong echo, as in a sort of "sounding board".

Luckily, associations and university research centres followed up my survey closely, and they provided tools to identify bot masses disguised among follower flows in different social media profiles.

Some web services like "Political Bot" or "Bot Check"[55] are just an example.

Over the years, and more than once, Twitter itself launched campaigns to identify and, in some cases, delete bot users or inactive users.

Botnets

When a propaganda agency is set to use bots to maximise the efficiency of its communication strategy, it can employ bots in various forms. Messages do not only serve as a sounding board, but also become real weapons of mass distraction.

During debate in social media, especially Twitter, Facebook or Forum, the person promoting propaganda content may want to distort, corrupt or undermine the rational debate, thus deciding to set off a botnet against

---

[55] https://botcheck.me/

some opponent's content or profile. This, in turn, will cause fierce discussions, flames and shitstorms of various kind. According to Renato Gabriele, founder of "Oohmm" (Observatory of Online Harassment and Media Manipulation), more than 50% of online and social network most 'heated' conversations are not caused by people, but automated account nets, used by those interested in influencing the debate when exchanges multiply.[56]

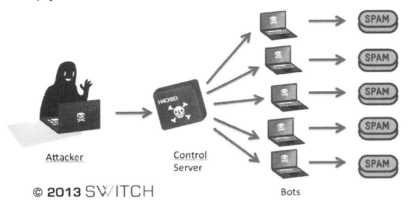

Attacker   Control Server   Bots

© 2013 SWITCH

Trump's staff used this botnet technique in 2015 elections, during the numerous "ad-personam" attacks against the figure of political opponent Hillary Clinton[57].
The alleged connection of botnets with Russian government or the rumoured turmoil over botnets belonging to Russia is, most likely, yet another fake news.

---

[56] https://oohmm.info/
[57] https://www.nytimes.com/2016/11/18/technology/automated-pro-trump-bots-overwhelmed-pro-clinton-messages-researchers-say.html

Twitter admitted that democratic candidate Clinton had received at least fifty thousand retweets by the presumed bot networks themselves, "retweeting" Trump content more than four hundred seventy thousand times, accounting for a total 4% of overall retweets obtained by the conservative candidate.

Bot localisation in Russian territories where these agencies provide such services is simply due to the fact that, many freelancers and programmers developing this type of algorithms are found in Russia, and their prices are way much cheaper than their English or American competitors.

Botnets and their use in social media have started a real black market where there are not only automatic software performing tasks, but also actual profiles voluntarily turning into bots.

BuzzFeed investigated thoroughly the phenomenon in the first months of 2018.

Journalist Alex Kantrowitz found out how many user communities get organised using social media marketing services, or even Telegram groups[58] to coordinate networks producing likes and comments, fooling Instagram.

Instagram algorithms cannot halt the process of fake Engagement against non-verified profiles.

With regards to this subject, in February 2018, Instagram channel "Viral Hippo", set up by BuzzFeed journalists,[59]

---

[58] Instant messaging service based on security and secrecy of conversations

[59] https://www.buzzfeed.com/alexkantrowitz/people-are-turning-their-

published some random and rather nonsensical pics (a black quadrant and a dark concrete block) reaching an exorbitant number of likes and some comments.

Many likes and comments came then from verified profiles, which were not genuinely interested in specific content, but rather using social media agencies like "Fuelgram".
Such agencies spread interactions on behalf of users to increase visibility, and in spite of the fact that this process is in clear breach of Instagram terms and conditions, no solutions have been found by service providers to stem the tide of this phenomenon.
We are looking at a market of Influencers and Native Advertising[60], whose reliability is potentially at jeopardy for a total value of half a billion dollars, already reached in 2017.
Following BuzzFeed survey, a great number of companies announced they want to look at the contract's effectiveness more closely.
Like most technologies, bots can be used in a more malicious way than cheating on the number of Followers or manipulating a debate. They can assume an almost "military" connotation.
For instance, botnets could be set to run various ethically debatable functions and manipulate discussion, or disrupt security systems and attack web services and providers.

Accounts-into-bots-on-instagram?utm_term=.yID6zqIRZ#.kcwbjZz6X
[60] Sponsored content published by influencers in own social media profiles or blogs

The term botnet can sometimes refer to computer devices infected by a particular type of malware, which enables hackers to manipulate a device to their liking.

Any kind of device can become a bot totally controlled by the felon hacker.

Currently, botnets may be made by hundred thousand zombie computers, and is currently ranking to be the main danger for computer safety today. Some botnets like "Mirai" and "Ramnit" were used between 2016 and 2017 to disrupt the operation of various worldwide web service providers and important banks.[61]

Named Botnets

Bagle	Conficker	Ozdok
Marina	Waledac	Kracken
orpig	Maazben	Festi
Storm	Onewordsub	Vulcanbot
Donbot	Gheg	LowSec
Cutwail	Nucrypt	TDL4
Akbot	Wopla	Zbot
Srizbi	Asprox	Kelihos
Lethic	Spamthru	Ramnit
Xarvester	Gumblar	Chameleon
Sality	BredoLab	**Mirai**
Mariposa	Grum	

61

http://www.repubblica.it/tecnologia/sicurezza/2015/02/25/news/cyber crime_smantellata_rete_che_ha_infettato_3_2_milioni_di_pc-108157604/

HOW FAKE NEWS IS CREATED

PREPARATION

Define objectives

During phase one, the person that I will call mystifier or polluter from now on, must define objectives that he/she aims to reach by spreading fake news.

Fake news is created to attain the media effect to favour or hurt a brand, person, promotion mechanism, public opinion, or a defined group of people, depending on context or customer's need.

If the objective is to influence public opinion, in general, polluter shall make sure he/she creates populist content capable of involving a very high number of people.

If the objective of the disinformation campaign is to influence specific people like decision-makers or similar, the editorial plan and methods of news distribution will differentiate according to requirement.

Polluter must always keep a clear objective in fake news campaigns, which is deemed necessary to evaluate the efficacy, the impact and the penetration fake news can have in traditional media.

Define public

Firstly, a polluter pursuing a given purpose has to define a specific audience, bearing in mind that fake news spread more easily if it goes viral in social media, traditional media or media hacking.

The polluter must operate within a frame of specific prejudice, pre-existing bias and false beliefs in order to ensure a high degree of involvement by target audience chosen.

Once audience is defined, the polluter will pick up a current topic upon which to base its news. News is then processed by using one or more logical fallacies to make it look different from reality and consistent with polluter's objectives.

.

With objectives defined and target audience chosen, polluter must decide which channels and tools to use to spread fake news. Some channels might be more suitable than others, depending on type of message or audience targeted.

The media hacker is in charge of news distribution through the various channels in social media and platforms, chosen to achieve desired effect.
Generalist social media allow a much larger audience, and they also spread more rapidly.
If fake news campaign targets a generalist public, not confined to a particular set of people, social networks like Facebook or Twitter are good enough.

On the contrary, if polluter is primarily focused on a vertical and specific audience, LinkedIn, with the use of Twitter lists, is the ideal environment to distribute fake news.

In some cases, it might be necessary to inform a person or decision-maker and influence this restricted and specific audience by representing or rather mystifying the interests of a vast public with the support of large figures.

Create content

Polluter must define topics in details and according to target audience. They must know how to develop and expand the cognitive bias which will reinforce the rhetoric of fake news.

The target audience is an increasingly better carrier of fake news the more controversial or emotionally charged the news is.

In politics, if the strategy is to steer up the moods and feelings of a specific right-wing constituency, for example, it will be advantageous to submit fake news that reinforces the content of racist, xenophobic and nationalistic beliefs.

Fake news reporting alleged crime, property damages, or violent behaviour by illegal immigrants will therefore be published for readers living in the proximity of migrant and refugee camps.

Sometimes, it will be sufficient to reach your audience with real and actual news, only selecting the news articles that unleash the biggest outrage in public opinion. The topic and/or problem will be perceived as much bigger than it really is.

The media bubble, commonly referred to, as 'filter bubble', generates similar effects to the practice described above. Excellent results can be reached by inserting fake news feed to the bubble.

The polluter will fuel up fake news regarding maxi salaries, benefits, annuities paid to civil service executives, and will send it to those who have recently lost their job, or generally live in high unemployment areas. He will publish news on non-existent rapes committed by illegal immigrants for a female audience; or fake news of alleged infant kidnappings by gypsies and roamers and so forth to parents and families.

The more fake news relies on popular beliefs the more credible it becomes.

The media hacker deals with fake content, text, articles or messages, but also multimedia images, graphs, pictures and videos.

Fake content will be accompanied by forged graphs, counterfeit data or fake multimedia attachments. Any image can be easily feigned, altered or counterfeit by manipulation of the EXIF data (Exchangeable Image File), in order to avoid the risk of fake debunking, after reverse image search in Google, or other editing software available.

Even audio-visual content like "Tensorflow" can be manipulated and counterfeited to create fake multimedia content with present artificial-intelligence technologies. This type of fake content, known as "DeepFakes", also helps promoting the fake news campaign.

In other words, it is possible to create words, meetings, or actions that never took place.

Draw your weapons

Polluter now needs to make its ready-packed and fake content look like real and delete any online evidence of its forgery. He needs to wrap up a believable story that can be easily found by fact checkers if searching the web. A website or a social network hosting the fake story could be set up accordingly.

Polluter also needs to arrange other things like ad-hoc technologies to spread fake news, false profiles, bots, botnet and advertising or social media marketing services. A team of people might be assembled to help promoting fake news since human resources can work in synergy with botnets or social media marketing services.

The team of people can add extra relevance and credibility to fake news content, divert attention as necessary, or disrupt rational debate during debunking.

Various web services come to the aid of polluter to disguise its IP address, (Internet address of computer connected to the web) and Proxy Servers or Tor networks (computer systems or applications used to avoid traceability) which are able to bypass even the most stringent blocks.

ACTION

Activate your weapons

Once fake content is disguised as real news, and media hacker has decided the specific technologies and resources to use to promote fake news, action begins.

The media hacker can now start spreading fake news via social media or text messaging services.

The right Claim (i.e. title announcing post) and the right Post preview can ensure remarkable results in the level of Engagement generated by the Post containing fake news.

Then, when fake news is spread via social media, it is also possible to target the audience according to a myriad of criteria, ranging from age group, level of education, geographic location and several behaviours and interactions stored in Facebook or Google advertising.

Targeting through social media can favour the spreading of a potentially complex editorial plan for fake news, *purposely* designed to chose the various targets to hit.

Immediately after the fake content publication, the media hacker gives way to the score calling for a high Engagement to the fake Post, also leveraging the so-called *"vanity metrics"*[62]. They contribute to the increase of the Post's authoritativeness and virality.

Social media tools make possible to monitor the systematic and structured results of spread content in real time.

Use your weapons

As already pointed out, artificial tools like bots and botnets are used to increase the progress and virality of fake   news.

Bots are in this case used to evoke a higher response to the fake content spread by media hacker, in terms of not only flow, pattern, retweets, shares, likes or comments, but also the attractiveness of content itself in the eyes of a real user[63].

Studies have proven that content becomes more interesting for the average user if it can involve a high number of people.

In this case, bots and botnets serve the purpose of giving fake news the emotional attractiveness necessary to captivate the average user's attention for a few extra seconds. Enticed by the content virality an average user will dwell longer to read the Post preview.

(See "Bandwagon" fallacies further on).

---

[63] https://insights.newscred.com/psychology-behind-viral-content/

The use of human resources in propagating fake news also concerns the generating of so-called *"flames"* whose side effects is to increase content virality.

Manipulated public outrage can frequently turn out to be more effective than seeking public opinion consent.

Cognitive hacking

Transmediality is the very nature of fake content.
If fake news or propaganda content is dispersed through the web first, it is also bound to produce media effects outside the online world, influencing our daily reality.
Orson Welles had already proven how traditional media (i.e. newspapers) could be manipulated by fake news with the introduction of a then new media, the radio.

Following the same process, the content of social media fake news ends up in printed magazines and daily newspapers, or TV news. The use of information, for all types of media, even traditional ones, goes through digital mechanisms every day.

A technique widely used in Character Assassination, (that we will explore later) is to create false online content, which not many people are likely to read, but which will be sent to end receiver by false profiles.

End receiver will perceive that a large number of web users 'overheat' with regards to this topic.

There were cases of false news created to defame a Professor by sending fake news to the web and artificially inflate news with likes and shares, which had never taken place.

The purpose was to deliver the fake news to the end receiver, the Dean. The perception was that the case was serious and widely known and this questioned the Professor's reputation.

In this case, the technique is accomplished by sending text messages and calls to the answering service or the secretary of targeted objective (the Dean).

Using botnets allows the automation of a number of actions, which do not pertain to digital communication and enter our daily tools instead. As an example, a botnet can be arranged with a very high number of phone calls to a specific phone number by using an algorithm designed for vocal traces.

There are other cases of "mental pitfalls" which imply the massive send out of mails and telephone text messages to simulate non-existent message chains and words of mouth.

Salve,
Per rinnovare WhatsApp
a costo di 0.89 bastera
cliccare questo link.
http://whatsapp-it.com/
subscribe/
o vostro WhatsApp verra
disattivato.

In the case of text messages, in particular, it is not unusual to come across fake messages that pretend to be official communications by a known service provider that, coincidentally, is soon to be at a charge, if we do not provide payment quickly.

These typical text messages called *"fishing"*, are devised to fool inept users and collect some pennies with this type of hogwash fraud. In this case, the ill-intentioned person purports to be a trustworthy body or office to try to obtain sensitive information, such as, personal or bank information, security codes etc. etc.

M.R.D.

Measure

As repeated many times, monitoring how fake news performs is extremely important for news mystifier/polluter. Google Analytics is one of the most common tool to measure performance in newly created or controlled websites. There are some relatively complex tools such as "Hootsuite" or "Talkwalker.com" that can analyse in-depth the interaction between users, groups of friends and the "social writing".

All these tools allow to monitor user traffic, in real time, and tracing user movements within the environments or sites where fake news circulates.

.

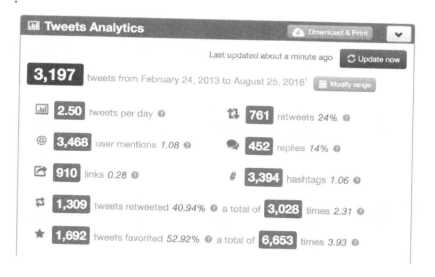

Replicate

Fake news never really walk alone and are often part of a bigger communication strategy, propaganda, or a money-making frame.

Monitoring and measuring the performance of fake news help smooth out some publishing or redistribution aspects inherent to fake news or other similar fake content.

Performance results of news first publication can contribute to how Promoters allocate budget. They may decide to spend more on fake content that showed a bigger capacity to reach users, or invest on vertical users that showed more involvement.

Defend

Lastly, it is fundamental to protect, as far as possible, fake content from Debunkers, Fact Checkers or the usual critical commentaries.

Every lie, sooner or later, is exposed, and, although there is only one reality, that truth will come to light, social media mechanisms that regulate Post virality cause fake news to become widespread a lot quicker than the subsequent debunking comment ever will.

The Brandolini's Law, firstly announced by Italian programmer Alberto Brandolini in 2013 asserted that the amount of energy required to fight fake news is measured on a much higher scale than what is needed to generate the fake news itself.

Essentially, fake news and hoaxes spread much faster than informative quality content.

We have described so far the numerous ways to create fake news and how to continuously defend fake news from debunking.

Some of these methods, aiming at disrupting the rational debate, have their roots in rhetoric and logic. These methods are brought up during production of fake news or content.

We will investigate some of these methods in the next chapter.

TECHNIQUES TO CONFUSE

We examine here the case of an agency that needs to create or spread online fake news to encourage propaganda on behalf of a customer.

Firstly, fake news must come from a website that looks like an actual magazine, newspaper or blog.

If agency does not have a communication channel to spread propaganda, it can set one up easily for that purpose. The agency will spend a few hundred dollars to buy a domain, maintain servers and acquire an online base presence (followers, likes and retweets on social networks).

This is an important step to make users believe to already possess an efficient network of influence and a solid online presence (followers, likes and retweets).

After creation of channel distribution for fake news, agency needs effective and addictive content, so that users can identify with the propaganda messages it supports.

To generate fake news you start from a current event or a topic already part of the public collective imagination.

Afterwards, you need to interpret facts in a fallacious way, to reach conclusions that reinforce the propaganda message.

If, during Brexit, an agency would have wanted to sustain the Leave Campaign with manipulated content, it could have started generating false news on immigrants supposedly committing crime all over England and causing the crime rate to increase in the island.

Alternatively, it could have supported the claim that surrendering English sovereignty to the European Union would have jeopardised British economic growth.

Regardless of the information veracity or falseness, fake newsmakers leverage a rather popular logic fallacy to entice the irrational section of a reader's mind by invoking popular beliefs, prejudice and common sense.
In some cases, it is a powerful and elaborate ruse of rhetoric and a brutal "ad personam" attack.

WHAT IS A LOGIC FALLACY?

Logical fallacies are errors and flaws hidden in reasoning. People who are so sure of their assertions and their rigour do not see the invalidity or faultiness of their argument, and, therefore, they commit a logical fallacy
The term "fallacious" refers to an invalid argument, rather different from not being true, which poses deductive, invalid or unacceptable links among propositions. Propositions could be "true" but the inference among them might be invalid or unacceptable.

Everybody agrees on the etymological origin of the word fallacy deriving from "fallere" which is the Latin verb for "deceive" or fail. Several writers and scholars of logic have attributed slightly different facets to the structure, origin and working of fallacies.

Faulty or invalid reasoning is usually done with the purpose to persuade or dissuade, convince or discredit, in a fraudulent and deceiving way, even unknowingly or unintentionally.

In spite of the conspicuous number of existing fallacies and in many cases bearing a strong similarity too, I tried to broadly divide fallacies into two big groups, and followed a rational order: formal logical fallacies and informal logical fallacies.

Formal logical fallacies

A formal logical fallacy (also called "deductive fallacy) is a faulty reasoning which presents an invalid logic structure. The structural invalidity of formal fallacies can be neatly explained with the reason arguments of classical logic.

Example
A person asserts: "Tuesdays are typical rainy days." There is no logic implication between days of the week and meteorological events.
It ensues that such statement is affirmed through the only individual and subjective perception of the person who cannot describe any logic inference between the two events, "rain" and "Tuesday".
The assertion is considered invalid then.

Informal logical fallacies

An informal logical fallacy is a type of fallacy that emerges when the argument is based on premises that do not have adequate "logic ground" to support the conclusion they draw.
The fallacy does not belong to the context of logic

structure, but it invalidates or makes false the premises used to derive the argument's conclusions.

Example

A person states that "in 2017 the invasion of refugees landing in UK coasts brought more than a million immigrants causing UK crime rate to rise by 3% compared to previous year.

Hence, immigration equals more crimes."

There is no proven "cause-effect" relation between the number of migrants in UK and crime increase. Any relationship or linkage must be proven and supported by evidence, and could, in no case, be the only factor determining the increased crime rate in the country. Therefore, the assertion turns out to be invalid.

Tylervigen.com is a website which allows selecting random events and correlating. It is possible to find a correlation between number of people drowning in swimming pools and movies where Nicholas cage has appeared in. Hence, we can generate any correlation to be used in politics, as an example, to prove something, which can be of political use.

THE CLASSIFICATION BY DAMER

There are various subcategories, taxonomic schemes and organisations of common logical fallacies encountered during reasoning.

Some of them date back to the great scholars of logic, or thinkers of the past like Aristotle, Francis Bacon or Immanuel Kant.

We chose to describe logical fallacies according to a modern classification by a US contemporary author and philosopher, who wrote a manual on the subject of logical fallacies in early 2000. "Attacking Faulty Reasoning[64]" is a textbook written by T. Edward Damer that thoroughly deals with logical errors. The textbook has been used in many college courses on logic, critical thinking, argumentation and theoretical philosophy for several years.

T. Edward Damer sets forth roughly 60 common fallacies when engaging in a debate and each fallacy is defined concisely and accompanied by relevant examples.

Organisation of fallacies derives straight from the author's theory of own fallacious arguments. He defines a fallacy as "any violation of the five criteria of a good argument.

The argument must be structurally well formed and the assertions must be relevant. The premises must be relevant and acceptable; sufficient in number, weight, and kind, to be effective in the process of rebuttal of challenges to the argument.

Every cognitive bias belongs, at least, to one of the five categories deriving from above criteria.

The first class of cognitive bias violate the sufficiency criterion. The sufficiency criterion requires that, one who argues for or against a position should use an argument that meets the fundamental sufficiency requirements of a well-formed argument.

---

[64] Damer, T. Edward. *Attacking faulty reasoning: a practical guide to fallacy-free arguments* (7th ed.). Boston, MA: Wadsworth, Cengage Learning.

In short, the reasons to validate the acceptance of a conclusion.

The second class of cognitive bias violate the structural criterion. The structural criterion requires that, one who argues for or against a position should use an argument that meets the fundamental structural criterion of a well-formed argument. The premises that are compatible with one another must not contradict the conclusion, assume the truth of the conclusion, and not be involved in any faulty deductive inference.

The third class of cognitive bias violate the relevance criterion which requires that, one who presents an argument for or against a position should attempt to use only the reasons that are directly related to the merit of the position at issue.

The fourth class of cognitive bias belongs to logical fallacies that violate the rebuttal criterion.
By analogy, it is required that, one who presents an argument for or against a position should provide effective rebuttal to all serious challenges to the argument and ensure the application within its theoretical structure.
It is also required to tackle the serious challenge to the argument or position supported, or a strongest argument for possible alternative positions.

Finally, the fifth class is logical fallacies that violate the acceptability criterion.

The acceptability criterion requires that, one who presents an argument for or against a position should attempt to use reasons that are likely to be accepted by a rationally mature person and that meet the standard criteria of acceptability.

Logical fallacies, which appeal to emotions, fall into this class.

The last type of logical fallacies is of primary rhetorical importance, also in reason of its frequent use in online communication and for the "Filter Bubble" effect that it produces.

In addition, the use of "Sentiment Analysis" by agencies extracting data from social networks, especially in politics, helps propaganda to be forged and divulged on the basis of beliefs, fears and prejudice.[65]

VIOLATING THE SUFFICIENCY CRITERION

Masked man

The masked man, or Leibniz's Law, as well as Red Herring, are widespread logical fallacies.

These fallacies consist in assuming that, if two objects do not have the same characteristics, in no case, they can be the same. There cannot be separate objects or entities that have all their properties in common.

---

[65] https://www.lindiceonline.com/osservatorio/economia-e-politica/elezioni-campagna-marketing-cross-mediale/

The 1700 philosopher, Gottfried Wilhelm Leibniz referred to the ontology of things, that is, "what things are in their true nature" and "the indiscernibility of two subjects".

When two subjects share every aspect, characteristic or attribute, they can be defined as "identical".
This assumption always refers to the condition of "be" and never of "know", since knowledge is a state which philosophers would call theoretical and not ontological.

For this reason, we end up in logical fails when we try to apply the principles of Leibniz's Law to facts pertaining to knowledge or information. The logical fault is determined by the presumption that our knowledge of a given event may unequivocally be the ontology of the event itself.

Consequently, our judgement or knowledge of an object, person or situation, cannot ever constitute the absolute and only truth.

Example
Lora Lane knows Clark Kent in his role of journalist very well, to the extent that she makes Clark believe she knows every detail of his life.
On the other hand, Lora does not know the real identity of Superman.
Given that Lora knows Clark's identity, but not Superman's, the inattentive reporter concludes that Superman cannot be Clark Kent.

Special pleading

The rhetorical technique consists in defending the argument's accusation and shifting the focus of discussion by evoking "special" or "unique" exceptions.

Admitting to be wrong, having championed and sustained a fallacious idea, and suddenly realising that your own argument has an unexpected fail, can produce an emotional pain which a human being will usually try to escape.

To avoid the unpleasant reality, that would unequivocally place us on the wrong side of the barricade, we look for tales that can justify our "false" or mystified position.

We invoke possible exceptions, which we entangle in our Storytelling to justify our mistaken position.

Beliefs and superstitions

Some ideas are intrinsically more liable to special pleading technique than others are.

Religious and mystical beliefs, if inclined to the world of the supernatural, tend to seek refuge in peculiar tales of fantasy when they are contradicted.

It might seem pleasant and thrilling to be part of a tale where one is described as the leading character of a story that does not obey any general and established logic, such as, natural laws, statistics or scientific rigour, whilst it will sound like "Special Pleading" to the listener.

Special Pleading" is a sort of final weapon, which the speaker uses as a last resort to shield the entity of its own idea being deconstructed.

A good example could be the phoney guru who claims its powers come to a standstill before the presence of a sceptic.
A famous Special Pleading found in the world of ancient philosophy is the alleged quote attributed to Saint Augustine. When asked what God was doing before the creation of paradise, to the sceptics who were clearly questioning the cosmology of the Christian philosopher, Saint Augustine would angrily reply as follows: "He was preparing hell for those asking such question".

Special pleading and fan-zone

Special Pleading may also become a special and particularly efficient means of persuasion and involvement to strengthen the connection among users of a specific group, either political, ideological or market area.
It is a means to convince users, voters or supporters to be an outstanding exception, part of a special group which rejects the general rules that afflict the rest, who are either more wicked, or less smart.

The advertising campaign carried out by Apple from 1997 to 2002 made an excellent use of the Special Pleading technique, summed up by the claim "Think Different" - which, just by the sound of it, made users feel part of a special community.

We here analyse the campaign wording:

Here's to the crazy ones.
The misfits.
The rebels.
The troublemakers.
The round pegs in the square holes.
The ones who see things differently.
They're   not   fond   of   rules.
And they have no respect for the status quo.
You can quote them, disagree with them,
glorify or vilify them.
About the only thing you can't do is ignore them.
Because they change things.
They push the human race forward.
While some may see them as the crazy ones,
we see genius.
Because the people who are crazy enough to think
they can change the world, are the ones who do.

The text quotes types of people who appear like a small group, but represent the "feelings" and "the way any person feels" by the large majority of people. Any and every person feels he/she is "crazy", "non-conformist", or "rebel" in his/her own way.

Who has not ever caused trouble? Who has ever been fond of rules? Who has ever loved a status quo?
The answer is anybody!

The wording was construed to emotionally embrace users and make them feel part of a group who is aware and proud of being different.

After embracing a large number of people with its initial call, the central section concentrates on one of the most common fears of human mind: be ignored, have no impact and pass unnoticed.

The advert assures that all people quoted can be glorified or vilified, but not ignored.

It concludes with the sentence that sums up the spirit of special pleading.

"Only those fool enough to think they can change the world, can really change it". If analysed according to a simple logic structure, the sentence could mean:

"If I am so fool to think I can really change things, then I can really change them. Because I am fool enough. Other might not understand me, but I am a genius and nobody can ignore me".

Anyone hearing such a conversation from a real person would think he/she is face to face with a mythomaniac person or an individual who wants to set up a sect of narcissists.

However, since the text was pronounced by one of the most important brand of the century, Apple words became a real cult and one of the most innovative and creative campaigns of all times.

It was so groundbreaking that 20 years later, Samsung, Apple's biggest competitor for smartphones, launched a campaign for its new model called "Upgrade to Samsung".

The video tells the story of a young man that has used an iPhone throughout his youth, believing it was the coolest choice, but once he is grown up and matured, he realises that it is time to "evolve" and abandon Apple device in a drawer to pass to Samsung.

Again, the Special Pleading technique and a personal recount are used to imply two different and inconsistent evaluation criteria to justify a story, an exception, or as in this case, the choice of a product.

Conjunction

The logical fallacy of "Conjunction" is based on the presumption that several specific conditions are more probable than a general condition.
The most mentioned example of this fallacy was created by Amos Tversky and Daniel Kahneman, two neuro-scientists and psychologists.

Linda's problem

Linda is 31 years old, single, sincere and very intelligent. She has a philosophy degree.
Always a passionate student of issues like discrimination and social class injustice, she has also participated to anti-nuclear demonstrations.

The audience or speaker are then asked which thesis is more likely.

1) Linda works for a bank
2) Linda is a bank employee and an activist who participates in feminist movements

The largest section of the public will theorize that option 2 is more likely and will believe that two or more specific conditions are more likely to happen than one general condition, although there is no relation between the second option, which refers to Linda's past as a student, and what Linda does in her current life.

Tversky and Kahneman say that most people experience this cognitive problem because they usually use a simple method of computation, called "representativeness heuristic".

What appears to be more "representative" than premises, also appears more probable, when, in fact, statistically, it is not.

Appeal to probability

A case of logical fallacy in conjunction fallacies is the case of a gambler who relies on "probability". It is assumed that, if a specific event has not occurred for a long time, is due to happen soon.

This is the typical logical fallacy of gamblers, bookmakers or those betting money at casinos.

Personal incredulity

It is a logic fallacy where the speaker rejects an objective fact or a true assertion because he/she is unable to understand it.

It is often frequent to discuss complex events, which are far from common knowledge during conversations.

The structure of this kind of fallacy entails that if something is true, it must be seen by an individual and, therefore, if subject "X" cannot be visualized or understood, it cannot be true.

Example

Mario is a physicist and when Anna watches a cartoon on space, he explains that sound is produced in space because there is matter that can propagate it.

Anna does not understand the notion of "void" and "matter" and she reaches the conclusion that what her older brother, Mario, is saying, is false.

Example in media

In summer of 2017, Nicholas Kristof, a notable opinion maker of the New York Times, published an article where he sustained that, 2017 could have been the best year in the history of humanity if a series of data on education and poverty were introduced. The number of poor people or people starving and unable to access education would decrease.

Although Kristof used real data from authoritative sources, readers could not fully comprehend the complexity of the world geopolitical condition to correctly interpret the American journalist's survey.

Readers committed a personal incredulity fault as they interpreted the survey according to their limited knowledge.

Religious beliefs

Some logical principles derived from religion, such as, Christian creationism, may sometimes condition rational debate.
Theories on creation of the universe, where God created man and the universe, are in stark contrast with those largely and commonly acknowledged by the scientific community.
Big Bang and Darwinism are the two theories that most contradict the personal incredulity logical fallacies of Christians.

For a devout Christian it is impossible to imagine that a single cell can develop into a human organism in the course of hundred millions years; or that the Earth and the solar system, our galaxy and all known universe might have originated from a primordial bang.

The burden of proof

This logical fallacy implies that a proposition is deemed true or false if it is impossible to prove its truthfulness or falseness.

An individual assumes a proposition to be true because it has not been proven false yet, or a proposition is assumed to be false because it has not been proven true yet.

It could be classed as "false dichotomy", since the third option, which is not considered, would be as follows: "no sufficient investigations were carried out to define ''x'' proposition true or false and any judgement should be suspended'".

Examples in politics

During the campaign for his elections, Donald Trump made a complaint to CNN journalists and claimed that he had been a victim of alleged electoral fraud favouring Hillary Clinton.

Trump wrote in Tweet: "What PROOF do you have Donald Trump did not suffer from millions of FRAUD votes? Journalists? Do your job!" //

Trump committed a fallacy arising from the inversion of the burden of proof. Since he did not have any evidence supporting his claim of fraud votes, the president decided to fight back journalists asking them to check that no electoral fraud had been committed. Subtly, he was implying and taking for granted fraud votes had taken place.

VIOLATING THE STRUCTURE CRITERION

Loaded question

This logical fallacy implies the use of a loaded question, which will lead the respondent to be seen as guilty, whatever the answers supplied.
The loaded question will derail rational debate because of its inner accusatorial nature that blemishes any answer supplied.

We take the example of two employees both applying for the Manager's position in the same company.

During a meeting with the head of HR, one employee asks the other with a libellous tone: "Hey Carl, are you still attending Alcohol Anonymous classes?".

It is inconsequential if Carl is attending classes to stay sober, or he does not even drink. The question is a misleading slander. Whatever Carl replies he will not be viewed highly by the head of HR who is coincidentally responsible for his promotion, now at risk.

Link a Youtube
https://youtu.be/L4Ld4ZeINZA?t=2m10s   (Trump   VS   Hillary) https://youtu.be/K8ce2s2tWRE (CNN)

Journalists love this type of fallacy in particular.

Politicians can quote and slander each other in their mutual monologues, but rarely interacts with one another providing answers to questions.

On the other hand, reporters love to harass interviewees, partially to search the scoop at all costs, but also depict the character by forcing the interpretation they have already figured out.

In May 1996, American TV reporter, Lesley Stahl posed a very famous loaded question to Madeleine Albright, then US Ambassador for UN.

She asked Albright, with reference to the UN sanctions to Iraq "We have heard that half a million children have died. I mean, that is more children than died in Hiroshima. And, you know, is the price worth it". //

Albright replied that it had been a very hard choice to make, but the price was worth it.

Later on, Albright withdrew her own statement and regrettably admitted that she had fallen into a rhetorical trap.

Cause-effect relationship

Another logical and commonly found fallacy refers to the notion of "correlation" and "cause-effect relation".

This logical fallacy is typically formulated with the pretence that, if X event took place, as a consequence of Y event, both occurrences hide a supposed correlation.

These type of logical fallacies are the basis point for various conspiracy or unscientific theories aiming at mystifying the concepts of correlation and cause-effect relation. Conclusions are drawn from single events which are not supported by statistically relevant, or objective and verifiable data.

We here analyse the concepts of "correlation" and "cause-effect relationship" to better understand how they are mystified and confused.

Correlation

Correlation is the existing linkage between two or more variables, which tend to change together, either negatively or positively.

Negative correlation implies that if a variable increases, the other (s) decreases.

Positive correlation is the exact contrary: if a variable increases, the others do the same.

A negative correlation is the one that can take place between stock and inflation rate in case of a sudden rise in prices.

This example shows three variables: the trend of the stock market, the inflation rate and the rise in prices.

We know that, if prices rise suddenly because of an increase in the inflation rate, then the market slows down.

Another example of positive correlation is the link occurring between market offer and demand.

If demand increases, then offer increases too.

When product sales perform better than expected (demand), companies have to increase production (offer).

Variables are strongly interconnected among them, due to several "environmental" factors, or reasons dependant on logic, statistics, natural laws, jurisprudence laws and the socio-cultural context.

Mystified and fallacious example

Fallacious and mystified examples are those where inconsistent data or variables are engaged, even if not related to the topic, but only to support and validate a claim.

"I can prove Nicolas Cage is an awful actor! With the increase of his appearances in movies, deaths by drowning in swimming pools have increased"[66].

Variables have no direct or indirect relation, however, if shown in a mystified graph chart, (we will explain why further on), they could even appear like a proof quality to inexperienced people.

The cause-effect relationship

The cause-effect relation does not imply that variables increase or decrease due to the effect they have on one another.
Indeed, a variable is the originary factor of the other variable.

---

[66] Nicolas Cage drowns in a swimming pool in one of his movies. Real data, crazy statistics, hilarious conclusions that experts call "spurious correlations". They are apparent connections among events with no cause relation. There is a Website collecting thousands of spurious correlations since the age of Miss America. They go along with number of murders with burning objects, sales of iPhone, and have same numbers as people dying from falling off the stairs.
See more at: http://www.rainews.it/dl/rainews/articoli/correlazioni-spurie-Nicolas-Cage-al-cinema-in-piscina-si-annega-Dati-veri-statistiche-pazze-conclusioni-esilaranti-41922b2a-84f7-4ff1-8363-2218e67bdd7d.html

A case of cause-effect relation is where X event occurs, and generates Y event, which would not take place in the absence of X event.
Example
When X fact is committed, a corresponding X penalty is given, which would never be pronounced if X fact had not happen.

Mystified example
In England, Brexit supporters have always claimed that joining the EU was the cause for the impoverishment of English middle class in the United Kingdom.
Farage wrote an article on this subject in the "Express": "The EU's open borders make us less safe. As a bureaucratic club it makes us poorer."

First, he made a rather common mistake: he confused a hypothetical and high level of correlation with a cause-effect relation. Besides, the open borders of the Schengen agreement had never reduced levels of security in the United Kingdom.

Other cases of mystified cause relation are found in the field of medicine and typically in the literature pertaining to its divulgation.
We here suppose the case of a child who is affected by a disease following his vaccination.
The disease could have been contracted because the child was predisposed, or for multiple causes where, in a remote and hardly verifiable instance, the vaccine could only be a contributory cause. It is wrong to identify the event "vaccination" with the cause of a given pathology.

This type of logical fallacy is defined by the Latin phrase "post quam, ergo propter quam", meaning after this, therefore, because of this".

The slippery slope

The rhetorical technique consists in presenting a series of conclusions as inevitable, after a fact is asserted and warranted by a party.

If an event takes place, it will lead to other events, suggesting their consequentiality despite the conclusions being totally arbitrary.

Example
A person affirms: "Legalising gay unions may lead to legalising incest one day, and therefore the future destruction of the family concept. This will result in the extinction of the human race. 'Legalising gay marriages is the first step to extinction".

This reasoning is victim of the slippery slope argument because it states the consequentiality of two or more facts as certain, (a generally negative effect) although they do not have an actual consequential link.
The logic succession applied is, in fact, totally arbitrary.

The way the slippery slope fallacy works can be summed up as follows.

If A is true, then B will happen. B will lead to C that will lead to D. Hence A = D.

Nonetheless, the actual relation between the two events is not proven, nor the inevitable consequentiality argued.

Origins

The slippery slope fallacy, as well as other cognitive bias, have their roots in the "perverted reasoning" of medieval and Aristotelian logic.

In this case, the logical fallacy that Edward Damer describes as "domino effect" in his book, is structured like a "modus tollens" reason, short for "modus tollendo tollens" meaning "that denies by denying"

It is a hypothetical syllogism whereby the second premise is a proposition whose truthfulness is not derived from deductive reason, but rather an 'evidence' or an empirical assumption.

Historians have looked closely into the study of hypothetical and disjunctive propositions.

Slippery Slope in politics

In politics or business, this rhetorical artifice is used by partisans of conservative positions to discredit advocates of progressive, reformist and change-oriented views.

Example

Faced with the proposal to remove the statues of the Great Confederacy Generals, a symbol of white race supremacy for many, President Trump declared that:

"Remove the beautiful statues of the Confederacy is silly: they are part of our history and roots. Our next step will be to take away the statues of George Washington and Thomas Jefferson".

President Trump is victim of the 'Domino Effect' explained by Damer. There is no connection between the removal of the confederacy statues and the removal of the statues dedicated to the founding fathers of the American country. However, Trump predicts a series of negative effects, deemed as inevitable.

Link youtube

https://youtu.be/c5QdzqbCxgl?t=7s

VIOLATING THE RELEVANCE CRITERION
Appeal to purity

The logical fallacy called "No true American" or appeal to purity, specifically redefines the judgement method used by someone who faces rebuttal of its entire argument.
The person who asserts a universally valued argument is committing a logical fallacy.
Faced with the rebuttal which proves the fallacy of its argument, the person redefines its judgement now asserting the argument is no longer in the universal

category he has supported or so far opposed, rather than admitting to be wrong.

Example
An old pizza maker, complaining about new, young cooking trends, says: "No true Italian would use ketchup in pizza". Carlos, an Italian with a Chilean family, replies: "I put ketchup in pizza but I am Italian". The old man replies with scorn: "You are no true Italian".

Origin of name
British philosopher, Antony Flew first introduced the term in his book titled "An Introduction to Western Philosophy: Ideas and Argument from Plato to Sartre", published in 1971.

In politics
President Trump and President Obama were both accused of logical fallacy, although for different reasons.

Obama was accused by Republicans to defend Muslim religion when he maintained that ISIS terrorists were no true Muslims.

High members of the Republican Party blamed Trump for not being "a real republican" or a "real conservative" and were gobsmacked to see his performance results at elections. Unable to identify with the new candidate, Republicans decided that Trump was not "enough of a Republican", blaming it on the President's ideological non-authenticity.

Identity problems

The logical fallacy is deeply connected with sense of identity or membership. It is intertwined with the emotions and beliefs of our affiliation to a group, ethnics, nationality, religion or ideology. The sense of identity can hugely condition and, in some cases, contaminate the rational debate.

The socio-political geographical and historical context where an individual conscience is formed will inevitably mould its theoretical ability and ways of using information.

This is the very reason why it is difficult for an individual to see (even own) opinions, clearly and objectively, regardless of own history and be exempt from, or go beyond cognitive bias. The sense of belonging makes it extremely complex to avoid the trap of logical fallacies, necessary to survive the sense of guilt for NOT belonging to a fallible group.

Link Youtube
https://youtu.be/BGjjwRL99fQ?t=45s

Anecdotal

Logical fallacies in all forms of anecdotal evidence manifest themselves with rebuttal of ascertained statements, regardless of any objectivity or scientific criteria, leveraging a single, casual and personal experience collected.

How it works

The anecdotal logical fallacy is a close neighbour of the confirmatory bias. It is structured as the need to deconstruct an argument based on scientific or statistical data, using the experience collected by a single individual or a small group of people and not based on any statistical method.

Cognitive bias victims, namely, confirmatory bias, are not inclined to understand the value of aggregate statistical data.

Examples

A classic example is the anecdotal logical fallacy referring to the presumed damages of smoking tobacco.

"Do you think smoking is bad for your health? My auntie used to smoke more than 40 cigarettes a day and lived up to 80 years old. Therefore, it is hard to agree with statistics according to which "smoking causes death in young people."

A young smoker will attempt to justify its addiction invoking the "anecdotal case" of his grandmother as opposed to million cases surveyed where scientific evidence proved it is evident that smoking damages health.

The young person does not understand that if his grandmother had not smoked, she could have lived longer or with a much better quality of life.

Surplus to say, that vaccine-related studies are conducted with scientific rigour and methods that proved autism is contracted because of many causal factors responsible for it.

The role of fake news

Every person has its favourite and particular way to recount a story to add more individual prominence and uniqueness to it.

An emotionally charged event, which one can identify with, makes it easy to turn reality into storytelling, removed from objectivity to become a subjective narration where one can be the undisputed leading character.

Web and social networks amplify this effect considerably. The social network bubble allows us to enter the subjective recount of reality of many people similar to us. We are led to the suggestion that, the sampling audience we are sharing our absurd beliefs with, is much bigger and significant than what it really is.

A vaccine opponent will normally browse "alternative" websites to search for information to reinforce its cognitive bias. He will join closed groups which propagate these types of fallacies.

Most of his social friends will share content from "feeds" supporting the logical fallacy to fuel up the spurious and specious argument. This will in turn originate a news bubble swarming with entirely subjective opinions and cognitive or confirmatory bias.

Link Youtube
https://youtu.be/L4Ld4ZeINZA?t=7s (Trump speech)

Confirmatory bias

The confirmation or confirmatory bias is a cognitive bias where people are inclined to use beliefs, knowledge or information that belong to their own frame of reference.

Origin
The confirmation bias was first discovered and tested in the course of some experiments carried out in the '60s by English psychologist, Peter Wason.

Brief traces that involved the mechanism of the confirmation prejudice were also found in ancient and classical literature.

Example

Saint Thomas Aquinas (a known scholar of Aristotle's logical studies) warned Italian poet and writer of the Divine Comedy, Dante Alighieri, that our ideas and opinions could move us onto the wrong side of the argument and even restrict the limits of our mind.

Arthur Schopenhauer, too, in "The World as Will and Representation" forewarns the reader from his own ideas, which he says: "tend to turn facts that support our argument into sparkling opinions and those which refute our argument into obnoxious opinions".

The way it works

The confirmation bias acts on the way an individual receives and processes information.

The effectiveness of the confirmation bias will determine how much the person is inclined to undervalue opinions other than his/hers and consequently overrate the ideas and opinions endorsing his/her argument.

Example

A right-wing voter tends to overestimate the opinions of intellectuals affiliated or endorsing the views of his party. On the contrary, he will express disdain for the academics or intelligentsia of the opposing party.

He will be interested in reading certain books and newspapers and will search for any proof to approve and validate his beliefs.

This repeated pattern, projected on a large-scale public opinion, will lead to the polarisation of ideas and opinions, an effect also greatly emphasised by the social media of our time.

VIOLATING THE REFUTABILITY CRITERION

Red herring

"Red herring" is the rhetorical artifice used to divert attention from the focus by means of an insignificant, marginal or inconsistent detail.

It is an actual element of "detour" placed in the discussion purposely to move the pivot of conversation onto trivial, inconsequential, deductive, but not accidental arguments. This pattern, in conjunction with totally useless details, will disperse the focus of problems to reach far-removed conclusions.

History

The most common use of the phrase "Red Herring" is nowadays connected with the technique of information manipulation, or in literary writing, it can refer to a sort of trickery where the author drives the reader towards a wrong conclusion. This type of ruse is often used in murder mystery or thriller stories.

The real origin of the Red Herring phrase boasts an ancient tradition though.

Legend has it that fox hunters used to smoke kippers, which would turn deep red with an intense and pungent smell to train hunting dogs follow the scent.

However, herrings were used at different stages of the dog's training. First, to initially teach puppies how to recognise and detect an unmistakable smell. Secondly, as an adult, the dog would be trained not only to improve its sense of smell, but also its attention, its concentration and its ability to sniff out "false tracks".

We must clarify that to recognise and rule out false tracks can turn into a factual cognitive exercise for human beings.
The "Red Herring" technique is applied to distract and lead astray from a problem, or a main critical issue of the conversation, often through the addition of a neglectable, detail, a superficial statement, or an ideological position potentially embraceable, but far-removed from the fulcrum of the debate.
Needless to say, it happens frequently in politics, marketing, propagandistic satire or fiction.

Example
A member of the government urged by an interviewer on a sensitive issue which would typically divide public opinion: immigration.
The politician would rather not express an opinion on the subject because it may reduce his/her popularity rate or jeopardize his/her audience appeal.
He will then shift the pivot of the conversation on a topic which diverts attention from the public.

"We will be able to control the migration flow to the best of our capacity, although what we care most, at the moment, is the political and financial stability in the areas concerned by the migration flow.

We will give our country adequate stability and suitable growth prospects."

Case history

During the debate against Hillary Clinton, when Donald Trump is urged to provide an answer with reference to the sexist comments leaked out of his video in 2005, he resorted to the "Red Herring" trick to wrong-foot everybody and kick the ball far away from the penalty box.

What ruse did the President use to move everybody's attention? He went as far afield as to mention the most known group of terrorists of the last years: ISIS.

Link Youtube

https://www.youtube.com/watch?v=f_ttbfTGs48
https://youtu.be/fXLTQi7vVsl?t=43s (From Obama's campaign)

Tu quoque

The "tu quoque" Latin phrase for "you also" or rhetorical technique "ad hominem" meaning to the man, (appeal to hypocrisy) is an informal fallacy that intends to discredit an argument and throws back the controversy to the person who started it. The fallacy points fingers to the person as the main responsible for the controversy itself.
It falls into the same category as the rhetorical technique called "ad hominem" (i.e. "to the man") and widely abused in political debates, news aiming at controversy and even in rulings by Courts of Common Law.

Origin
Julius Caesar when faced to his assassin notoriously pronounced those words. He famously uttered: "tu quoque Bruto, fili mi", meaning "you also, my son".
The tale was handed down by Suetonius and made famous by William Shakespeare in his tragedy entitled to Julius   Caesar.

Link youtube

https://youtu.be/1_sMyklCRhk?t=36s   (Friends)
https://youtu.be/L4Ld4ZelNZA?t=1m8s   (Trump   and Hillary Debate)

Ad personam

Rhetorical techniques called "ad personam" belong to the class of logical fallacies where sophistic theories very often aim at discrediting a speaker, or public audience, or trying to undermine the peaceful debate.

They can be generally classified into three main types: direct, circumstantial or "poisoning the well" techniques.

The first type could be defined as a common invective, which may turn into insult, depending on the extent of lewdness or the tone of elegance applied by the speaker. It is also known as "Ad Hominem", meaning to the man when it turns into an insult.

Pressuring someone by saying: "You believe vaccines cause autism because you are nothing but an idiot" is an invective against the person ("ad personam").

On the contrary, if you assert: "Anyone believing vaccines are harmful is undoubtedly an idiot," reflects the technique called "poisoning the well", that is to discredit an idea with pre-emptive prejudice, and present it to an audience which will or will not decide to champion the ridiculed or vilified idea.

If one would intend to apply the same principle of using invective, to rebut the argument, one could say: "You sponsor the use of vaccines because your wife works for a drug company". This would be referred to as an "ad personam" circumstantial rhetorical technique.

To sum it up, the case of the 'ad personam" invective occurs when the speaker is directly discredited, whilst the circumstantial invective refers to a personal fact, or a fact related to the life of the speaker. This last case assumes the cause-relation effect between the object of controversy and the personal fact brought up.

The "tu quoque"or "you also" belongs to the family of the rhetorical circumstantial techniques "ad personam", meaning "to the person".

These techniques refer to a fact or circumstance where the speaker is accused of lacking in consistency.

Example

"You affirm that addiction from psychotropic substances is a potential damage to public health, but I remember your youth revelry far too well!"

The two events asserting, "Psychotropic substances may cause damage to public health" and "the previous use of substances during youth" (assuming that the allegation were true), are, in no way, connected by causal link. Therefore, the argument has the sole purpose to cast aspersions on the initial argument.

Denigration takes place when an irrelevant event is called up and it can compromise the speaker's credibility, or the feeling of trust the public has placed in the speaker.

Link Youtube
https://youtu.be/c5QdzqbCxgI?t=2m25s   (Obama   on Sarah Palin)

Straw man

The Straw Man is a logical fallacy that envisages the fabrication of a "dummy argument" that can be easily attacked in place of the original argument.

The Straw Man fallacy, in addition to being one of the most diffused, is also one of the most complex and with more variables, on the ground that there are numerous ways and possibilities to construct a "dummy" argument.

Origin

The Straw Man assumes its current meaning associated to logical fallacies only in the early second half of 1900.
Douglas Neil Walton, a Canadian expert on information logic and logical fallacies, claims that Stuart Chase, an American economist and writer, was the first to use the expression "Straw Man" in his "Guides to Straight Thinking".

However, an English writer by the name of Thomas de Quincey had previously cited the expression "Straw of Man" in his works published in 1700.

Although the exact origin of the term is uncertain, it is likely that the phrase was related to the practice of combat training, which was performed by hitting a dummy, rather than a human body.

How Straw Man is formulated

The rhetorical technique of Straw Man consists in creating a weak, ad-hoc argument to substitute the main argument.

The weak argument must have some relevance with the main argument, so that the speaker can manipulate the respondent's attention to the extent that he can divert discussion to the 'dummy' argument quickly and easily.

The dummy argument can obviously take many shapes and forms.

- Push initial argument to the extreme
- Quote partial sections of out-of-context initial argument
- Include a person who defends mildly the initial argument and refutes the weakest defence. This gives the impression that initial argument is also being refuted
- Cite examples of emotionally-charged, borderline cases
- Mention events occurred sporadically and/or accidentally and present them as the norm
- Force analogies among arguments only apparently connected
- Oversimplify initial argument
- Come up with a fictitious character whose easily disputable ideas and opinions purport that the person defending the initial argument also shares the views of the fictitious character

Link Youtube
https://youtu.be/L4Ld4ZeINZA?t=2m45s

Bandwagon

Also known as "argument to the people", this bandwagon fallacy involves the ideological conditioning by a vast group, intended to be "the majority".

In the logical fallacy of the "argument to the people", a given proposition is presumed to be true or false by virtue of the fact that "the majority of people" believe it to be true.

The origin of the term

It refers to the "wagon" generally carrying a band of criminals, evildoers or salesmen, during the running of a parade or other entertainment events.

The phrase "jumping on the bandwagon" first appeared in American politics in the second half of the 19th century.

Dan Rice, a famous performer of the time, used his bandwagon to catch attention on his electoral campaign.

Later in early 1900, the bandwagon became the standard form of transport used in American political campaigns.

The expression "jump on the bandwagon" generally indicates a negative connotation, given that it refers to the attitude of those seeking approval or power without too much worry of how own name or reputation is associated to it.

The intellectual dangerousness of beliefs and the Bandwagon effect

It is an extremely common logical fallacy, found in multiple cultures and characterised by many facets.

The Chinese proverb "three men make a tiger" encompasses the same meaning of this rhetorical technique.

Bandwagon may refer not only to ideas supported by the majority of people, but also beliefs and superstitions in the cultural and religious legacy of a country.

The belief that bad people will be punished by some sort of divine justice is, for example, a bandwagon of Christianity.

The idea that monarchy is a form of government, which necessarily implies tyranny, is a cultural legacy produced by the Bandwagon effect from the Enlightenment period.

Many forms of prejudice and pseudo-racism are additional fallacious reasoning, in the same league as Bandwagon.

As an example, the act of holding your bag firmly in the underground when a person of colour passes you by, is not a sign of caution, but a Bandwagon effect. People of colour might be more prone to commit crime, as they are generally poorer.

It is the same belief as the prejudice to assume any person professing Islamism is a potential radicalized Muslim.

Various tragedies in human histories have derived from the devastating effects of Bandwagon.

From Jewish genocide, horrendously justified by the spreading of Nazi sentiment, the genocide that pretended

163

to civilise American Indians, to reach racial segregation in South Africa or USA in our days, based on the supposed supremacy of the "white" race over the supposed "black" race.

In social media

Filling up Facebook pages or Twitter profiles with fake followers is a standard practice to aim at bandwagon effect. The purpose is to attract real followers to a page that would otherwise pass unnoticed if real followers did not see a large and consistent audience. It is a therefore a logical fallacy, whereby users would not be induced to join without the bandwagon effect.

In economy

Economy is also affected by the Bandwagon effect.
It occurs when the number of people interested in buying a given good increases with the rising number of people buying it.
In summer 2017, Bitcoin and other cryptocurrencies rode the wave of Bandwagon, triggering a deep interest in cryptocurrencies, as well as Blockchain technologies.

In medicine

We could define Bandwagon in medicine as the "victory and acceptation of unverified, but very popular ideas".
Any "grandmother" old remedy, or some "traditional" and so-called "natural" medications belong to the group of Bandwagon effects. All adverts and propaganda messages are steeped in Bandwagon.

Make people believe that a huge majority has chosen to buy a product is of great importance for a company. Oral B has claimed its toothbrush is the most used product by dentists for years.

Are we really sure Oral B toothbrush is the best, only because it is used by the majority of dentists? No, we are not.

However, the message is captivating and interesting enough to ensure Oral B its desired market positioning in the eyes of its customers.

In politics

Every day, in TV or media, politicians and debaters invoke the public common sense.

Populism in the first half of our century was laced with campaign slogans, which have tipped or flirted with the Bandwagon effect.

"Politicians are all the same. They are all corrupt".

Bandwagon effects also happen for geographical or temporary reasons.

Few weeks after the victory of Brexit referendum, anti-European parties of other countries rose significantly in survey polls.

Similarly, during American elections, the Bandwagon effect influenced as a result of time differences in each US state.

When the East coast finished voting and started counting, the West coast was expressing its choice and polls were still open.

East coast results would have inevitably influenced votes underway in the West coast.

In 1980, the Press, many hours before voting finished in the West coast, proclaimed Ronald Reagan President of the United States of America.

Link Youtube

https://youtu.be/Pe7W827462o?t=3m27s (Trump)
https://youtu.be/fXLTQi7vVsl?t=2m57s (MSNB on Obama)
https://youtu.be/HaiCF8Vt6ec?t=23s (Nike commercial)

VIOLATING THE ACCEPTABILITY CRITERION

False dichotomy

Also referred to as a "Black or White", this logical fallacy presents a false dichotomy when in reality several nuances and options exist between two different opposites.

It is used to exacerbate two different positions and force a choice, or reinforce a position.

During invectives, political or public debates, and talks in general, this technique becomes a tool to urge and put the "thumbscrew" on the interviewee.

Expressions like "with or without me", "either you love or hate it", "stay or go", are all perfect examples of false dichotomies, used as a rhetorical artifice to force a position or decision.

Link Youtube

Either/Or

The either/or false dichotomy entails the oversimplification of a fact or event, to the extent that the last two remaining possibilities become two mutually exclusive alternatives.

Example
During a debate on migrants, a candidate is in favour of welcoming migrants to reception centres, whereas the other supports national border closure and expulsion.
The anti-migrant candidate will only support two options: send migrants back to their country of origin, or let them in to cause havoc to population.
The candidate in support of a fair reception will say the issue is more complex than what his colleague is suggesting. The other candidate will retort by introducing another false dichotomy: "There is no such thing as a complex issue"; either "you can explain things easily or you have not fully understood the issue".

In politics
In view of its great effectiveness, this rhetorical technique is largely used in political debates and any politics-related circle.

Regimes have long been known for their use of false dichotomies, such as, the notorious "With Reich or an Enemy of the Reich". However, democracies too are no stranger to using this type of fallacy.

Example

In 2015, with the objective to endorse the decision to sign an agreement with the Iran government, Obama and his entourage insisted that there were only two options to choose from, to sign the historic nuclear agreement: either to sign or prepare for war.

Democrats were highly criticised for the methods used to conduct debate on the agreement.

A few days after signing, Frederick W. Kagan, Director of the "Critical Threats Project" by the American Enterprise Institute exposed the Obama's "Black or White" rhetorical diktat in the columns of the " Washington Post".

Two years later, President Trump stepped back from nuclear agreement, again, using a false dichotomy.

In the course of a very critical speech against the Iran regime, Trump stated: "Either you fight terrorists, or you make deals with them. I want to fight them".

Link Youtube

https://youtu.be/Pe7W827462o?t=42s (Trump speech)

False compromise

Middle ground (or false compromise) is a logical fallacy that disagrees with false dichotomy. The middle ground fallacy concludes that, between two contrary and opposed opinions, the truth must lie somewhere in between, a compromise between two opposites.

To quote Aristotle, "in medio est virtus" meaning the "virtue stands in the middle". In fact, truth often lies somewhere in between two contrasting opinions.

Nonetheless, there are instances where it is not a question of two diametrically opposed opinions, but rather, one true statement and one false statement.

Example

Anna believes vaccines cause autism.

Roberto, an immunologist, believes vaccines do not cause autism in any way.

Veronica then concludes that the assertion most likely to be true is "vaccines may sometimes cause autism". She confuses a fallacious statement with a legitimate opinion. She has opted for an intellectual compromise, whereas all she needed was to refute or debunk the fallacious opinion.

Ambiguity

The logical fallacy of ambiguity consists in drawing a conclusion based on a premise likely to be interpreted with ambiguity.

There are different types of ambiguity fallacies, dependent on how the ambiguity element is structured.

Fallacy of Amphiboly

It is a logical fallacy of ambiguity where, either grammar, punctuation or words may be the cause for argument equivocation.

Example
"I am against taxation slowing down the economy".
Is the speaker opposing any kind of tax or just those which slow down the economy?

Fallacy of Accent

This type of fallacy implies that words in a sentence are ordered so that the message stresses certain words rather than others.

Example
"There will be no investments on my part for this year".
The emphasis of "no investments" aims at stressing there will be no financial efforts on the speaker's part, whilst the "my part" indicates the possibility of other investors.
On the contrary, if the accent is placed on "this year", the speaker is highlighting the fact that it is an event limited to the present year and there could be new investments in the future.

Use in advertising
Advertising often use this type of fallacy to emphasize some aspects of the product. Think of advertising boards

displaying messages written with enlarged characters to stress a concept, even if misleading.

To catch a customer's attention a pub might display a board outside its premises, saying "FREE BEER" and, underneath, in small characters, "after 8pm".
The text itself is not inaccurate or fallacious, but the word order is misleading.

Semantic misunderstanding

It is a proposition that carries a word or a phrase bearing two or more meanings of semantic understanding, maybe even two completely different meanings.

Example
"Some people have faith in the Church and others in Science."
This proposition contains semantic misunderstanding.
The word "faith" in religion presumes the belief in a spiritual or supreme entity.
The New Testament says that Jesus resurrects on the third day. I have no idea how someone could resurrect, but I have faith and therefore I believe it."
Faith in science instead, is intended as "trust", a feeling of authoritativeness and respect earned with time, and well deserved too.
Science provides proof and evidence in support of its claims and therefore we cannot speak of "faith". On the contrary, it is a sentiment of trust, an acknowledgement of intellectual respect and authoritativeness.

171

Illicit "observation"

This type of logical fallacy is similar to the misunderstanding where two words are contrasted as opposite, when in reality one is not adversary to the other.

Example

"They were incompetent politicians, but we will be honest!" The speaker is alleging that opponents were ineffective politicians, but, to mark his position, he is contrasting with a value, such as, honesty, irrelevant to the premise.

The opposite of an incompetent politician is a skilled or competent politician.

Honesty is not necessarily a value in contrast with incompetence in politics.

Quote mining

Quote mining is a logical fallacy which uses an out-of-context quote to validate an argument or a thesis.

A sentence removed from context can assume a different meaning and, in some cases, even an opposite meaning.

Hence, it would be advisable to avoid the use of quotes and citations out of their context of reference, unless one is absolutely sure the meaning is consistent with the frame used.

Phantom distinction

It is an informal logical fallacy of ambiguity, strictly connected with the Straw Man logical fallacies, but the exact opposite of semantic misunderstanding.

With a pedantic approach, the speaker decides to stress the accent on the distinction between two words, presented as synonyms or antonyms. (The distinction is perfectly useless to the rational debate).

Example

A: What is your opinion on the government's latest decision?

B: It is not a decision. It is a bill of law.

A wanted to know B's opinion on current news with regards to politics, whilst B has decided to rebut with a legal jargon subtlety, rather than give his opinion on the subject and supply an answer to A.

Wronger than wrong

There are no intermediate degrees between right or wrong in this logical fallacy. Any "false" proposition is equated to the same level of other false propositions.

Example

The belief that the Earth is flat is wrong.

The belief that the Earth is spherical is also wrong because the Earth is an actual oblate spheroid, almost oval, flattened at the poles and bulging out at the Equator.

However, the assertion that a spherical Earth and a flat Earth are equally wrong, is wronger than both those errors combined. It is a logical fallacy because there are different degrees of wrong. The image of a spherical Earth is undoubtedly closer to reality than the image of a flat Earth.

Moral equivalence

Moral equivalence is a rhetorical artifice, which pretends to compare two events of different importance from a moral standpoint, and seek to draw comparisons among them.

Events must be both necessarily relevant and different at the same time, to induce listener to believe that the two events have an identical positive or negative impact, although they are of different importance.

Moral equivalence generally trots out huge atrocities or the great conquests of humanity, to effectively leverage the highest emotionalism possible.

"As bad as"

To say that "reception centres for migrants can be compared to Nazi concentration camps", is in itself already an example of Moral Equivalence.

Concentration camps had a totally different purpose from reception centres built for migrants.

To draw such comparison equals to discredit the actual conditions of reception centres by comparing them to the Nazi atrocities known worldwide.

By analogy, saying that "there were no moral distinctions among Second World War factions since they all killed countless victims, (the German in the concentration camps and the American with the nuclear bomb) is a logical fallacy of moral equivalence.

The intent behind the horrific violent acts perpetrated during the war was deeply different. The Germans murdered million people for their insane theories on the white race supremacy, which put Europe at risk, and they waged war. The Americans always claimed they dropped the Hiroshima bomb to end the war, in retaliation to Japan's unwillingness to surrender.

''As good as''
The positive application of moral equivalence occurs when the purpose is to endorse an idea by drawing a comparison with an event whose impact was much more positive than negative.

Example
"The introduction of a citizenship income benefit is as important as the right to education".
Surplus to say that, it is more important to have access to schools, culture and academic studies, than to be paid a citizenship benefit.
Actually, the right to education is the fundamental basis of democracy and its principles, whilst the entitlement to citizenship benefit is a privilege of some advanced and rich democracies.

Fallacy of Composition

The fallacy of composition indiscriminately attributes a given characteristic to a group, and acknowledges it to a single part.
It ensues that, the total quality of an object is mistakenly defined based on the quality of its elements. This fallacy follows the fallacious form of a syllogistic verbal structure.

Example
Some parts in tanks can be lightweight.
Hence, tanks are lightweight.

The hoc mode

This is an informal fallacy according to which all that exists is based on the properties, which compose it, or the matter, which constitutes it. The fallacy does not admit any difference in the method of composing matter or the order to arrange its properties.

Example
A living and healthy calf and a butchered calf are made of the same matter, but the arrangement and composition of the matter between the two calves change substantially. Therefore, the two calves are not the same thing.

Apex

This is a specific variation of the fallacy of composition where the experience or performance of best group members conditions the qualitative attribution of the whole group.

Example
Men hold the majority of executive offices.

To say there is gender equality will be a logic fault, conditioned by the performance of a group.

Following the same dialectic, we could say society has developed a problem of gender discrimination because prisons are flowing with men.

The paradox of Thrift

This fallacy of composition occurs in some subject matters, which involve the use of logic, like economy.

The paradox of Thrift is one of the pivotal conundrum of Keynesian economics. Keynes shifts the focus of economics from output to demand, and argues that, in some specific circumstances, aggregate demand is not sufficient to guarantee adequate levels of employment.

Keynes affirms that, an act of individual saving (decrease of demand) will correspond to a rise in prices (aggregate decrease in demand). He concludes that the totality of acts of "Income" should always equal the totality of acts of "Outcome".

Example

To reduce general expenses a household family cuts its weekly dinners at the restaurant.

Therefore, the restaurant owner has to eliminate the cost of "Live Music" from entertainment.

The performer will be paid an evening less, and will consequently give up a weekly haircut at his usual barbershop, who coincidentally belongs to the head of the household who initiated the cost-cutting action.

Hasty generalization

The fallacy of composition is often confused with the hasty generalization fallacy.

They both share the same syllogistic structure where premises are true. Hence, the assertion is true.

However the difference lies in the type of premises chosen.

The fallacy of composition attributes a quality to a part of the group and the quality is true and verifiable whilst the fallacy of generalization (or fallacy of argument from small numbers) starts from a premise based on a small sample, often a personal experience or belief.

It does not have any scientific, certified or proven truthfulness.

A person saying: "I do not know who it was, but burglars broke into my house and it must be some of those gypsies living in the nearby campsite. All gypsies are burglars"

This sentence is not a logical error due to the fallacy of composition since the quality attribution of "burglar" to the presumed gypsy has not been verified to start with.

In case the attribution were true, it would not have any statistic relevance. It would fall into a subjective, statistically marginal range of cases, which constitute a belief rather than a verifiable statement.

Generalizations often pose populist, racist, prejudiced and indifferent statements as a premise.

Link Youtube
https://youtu.be/c5QdzqbCxgl?t=46s (commercial)
https://youtu.be/6v8vnTINzDk?t=22s (Trump on media's dishonesty)
https://youtu.be/fXLTQi7vVsI?t=5m31s (Mrs. Quaely 1992 Convention)

Texas sharpshooter

This logical fallacy consists in taking a specific cluster of data or statistics out of their own context, to bear out and validate a statement.

The name traces back to a joke whose main character was a man from Texas, who decides to fire shots against the walls of a barn. He then draws a target around the closest shots to brag about his ability as a sharpshooter.

German philosopher, Karl Popper, quoted this type of fallacy affirming as follows: "A theory that explains everything, does not explain anything".

He argues that any and every event could be interpreted as a tool to the reinforcement of a theory, and any possible implication by a third event proves useless to the rational argument.

This logical fallacy shares the same structure as the confirmation bias since it violates the relevance criterion, as well as the acceptability criterion.

The hasty generalization fallacy is widely used by lovers of conspiracy theories or pseudo-scientific thesis based on data clusters taken out of context, or allegedly "secret/supernatural combinations" of data.

Example

According to a study by Sugarette Drink manufacturers, it was pointed out that Sugarette products sell more in countries, which are rich, or with a highly positive health rate, compared to countries where product sales are lower.

They draw the conclusion that Sugarette drinks are good for health.

Link Youtube

https://bit.ly/2KXj8KN (Trump speech on Louisiana vote)

Fallacy of Division

This fallacy is the converse of the fallacy of composition. It extends the group's attribution of a quality to a single "part". If something is true for the whole must also be true for all or some of its parts.

Example

To affirm that a house is half the size of other houses in the area and therefore its entrance door will be half the size of other doors, is a logical fallacy of division.

In ancient philosophy

The logical fallacy of division was already addressed in Aristotle's works "Sophistical Refutations".

According to the writings of Lucretius, the Greek philosopher Anaxagoras was among the first to be victim of the fallacy of division.

He was one of the founder of Homoeomeria, a doctrine where the atoms constituting a substance, share the same qualities of the substance.

For Anaxagoras the atoms of water are wet, the atoms of fire are hot and so forth.

Begging the question

It is a fallacious reasoning where the argument's premises, implicitly or explicitly, assume the truth of the conclusions.

The premise is used to support itself and the conclusion is taken for granted, whilst in logical reasoning the truth contained in the premise must be proven.

The term is derived from a Latin expression, which can be translated as "assuming the initial point".

The unscientific language

This is a logical fallacy often encountered in pseudo-scientific or unscientific debates, which are frequently filled with claims whose truthfulness is not acceptable. The assertions are presented as premises in any case.

Example

«The scientific reason explaining why it is not possible to scientifically prove supernatural powers is to be found in the psi-negative mark that inhibits these powers and manifests itself in the event of scientific experiments with the supernatural»

The example is implicitly admitting the supernatural powers and the existence of the psi-negative mark, a supposed principle which inhibits the superpowers before scientific   evidence.

Although the assertion might show some kind of inner consistency, it is not acceptable because it presents some untrue and unverified premises as a fundamental basis of its argument.

Diallele or circular reasoning

'Diallele' is a word derived from ancient Greek (diállēlos, "mutual reasoning") meaning circular reasoning.

Circular reasoning is a rhetorical artifice used by classical logic to indicate a fallacious logical reasoning.

In circular reasoning, the initial premises derive from the consequences and the consequences are supported by the premises.

A vicious circle is so structured where no useful information is shared. It is the most common form of logical fallacies using the "circular cause and consequence" where the truth of the proposition is only apparent.

Example

"Women should be free to stop an unwanted pregnancy and therefore abortion should be legal". The premise "women should be free to stop an unwanted pregnancy" is already beginning with what it ends. The consequence of the proposition is summed up as being true and logical and "therefore abortion should be legal".

THE BRAIN IS THE MOST IMPORTANT ORGAN YOU HAVE

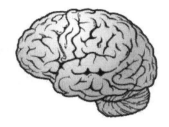

ACCORDING TO THE BRAIN.

The Cartesian origin

Criticism to circular reasoning has its first roots in the critic to the work of René Descartes called "Meditations of First Philosophy". He based his thoughts on an apparently circular reasoning.

« The thought that proves God and God that proves the thought»

- The idea of God is perfect and, hence, true, because it is clear and distinct (A)
- It finds its correspondence in reality, that is, the existence of a perfect and truthful God (B)

--->Hence A justifies B

- However, René Descartes used the proof of a perfect, good and truthful God to contrast this assumed truth and doubt the existence of an evil demon who generates a deceitful and illusory reality (B).

Antoine Arnauld was among the staunchest critics of the Cartesian logical error in circular reasoning.

In regards to the Cartesian circle, Antoine Arnauld stated as follows:

«I do not know how Descartes assumes he is not committing a circular reasoning when he says we are not sure that the things we clearly and distinctly understand are true, if not for the reason that God exists".

Arnauld is therefore deducing that we cannot be sure that God is, if we do not understand him clearly and distinctly. Before being sure of God's existence we must be sure that, the things we clearly and distinctly understand, are true».

Descartes replied by counterpoising the circular reasoning which uses the consequences of a thought to justify and further validate the same initial premises where doubts originated.

Link Youtube
https://bit.ly/2IObqWX

SYLLOGISTIC FALLACIES

Syllogism is a fundamental type of deductive reasoning in Aristotle's logic.

Syllogism is made by a major premise, either affirmative or negative, a minor premise and a conclusion necessarily drawn from premises. According to critics of syllogistic logic, there is actually a circular logic fallacy in every syllogism, or simply an assumption of the initial point, like the 'begging the question' logical fallacy.

We can conclude by saying that, if the syllogistic structure conforms to the principles of clarity, veracity and verifiability, it provides perfectly rational arguments.

On the contrary, fallacious arguments occur when the criterion of acceptability is disrupted.

We enclose some examples of syllogistic logical fallacies below.

Fallacy of the four terms

The first rule of syllogism applies the principle that there are only three terms: major, minor and medium. A fourth, or even fifth term, is not allowed as this would be called "the fallacy of the four terms".

Example
"Every fish swims", "Some constellations are fish", then "Some constellations swim". The term 'fish' is used with

two different meanings; we do not have three distinct terms, but four.

Illicit treatment of term (minor or major)
The second law of syllogism implies that the minor term and the major term must be distributed equally in premises and conclusion.

If the term distributed in premises was intended with a different meaning from the term of the conclusion, it would be a fallacy of illicit major or illicit minor.

Both fallacies could be considered as part of the same category "of the four terms", since the term distributed in the premises and the term of the conclusion are no longer the same, but there are four different terms.

Example
"All men are animals", "No horse is a man" and then "No horse is an animal".
The term 'animal' is said to be undistributed in the major premise, but it is distributed in the conclusion.

"All nihilists are dangerous", "All nihilists are critical", then, "All critics are dangerous". The term "critical" is not distributed in the minor premise, but it is distributed in the conclusion.

Fallacy of middle term

The third law of syllogism says that the middle term must not be distributed in the conclusion, since this type of fallacy would belong to the category of fallacies of the middle term.

Example

"All Athenians are Greek", "Some Athenians are philosophers", then "Some philosophers are Athenians" The rational conclusion in this case should be: "Some philosophers are Greek".

The undistributed middle term

The fourth law of syllogism indicates that the middle term must be distributed, at least, in one of the premises. If that is not the case, and the middle term does no longer connect the two terms, it is called fallacy of the undistributed middle term. The two terms could be included in subcategories other than the class appointed by the middle term.

Example

"All men are mammals", "All lions are mammals", then, "All men are lions"
The category of men and the category of lions are disjunctive subcategories of the class of mammals.
It is ensued that, the middle term ''mammals'' has no correlation with the major term ''elephant'' and the minor term ''mouse'''.

Negative premises

The fifth rule of syllogism implies that from two negative premises no conclusion can be drawn. The fact that two premises are not jointly related to a third premise does not necessarily imply that no link is established between them.

Example
"No fish is a mammal", "No reptile is a fish", and then "No reptile is a mammal".

Affirmative premises

It is the case of two affirmative premises and a negative conclusion. The sixth law of syllogism says that two affirmative premises can only reach an affirmative conclusion.
If either premises are positively connected to the same middle term, they must also be positively connected in the conclusion.

Example
"All animals differ from angels", "All men are animals", then "No man is an angel".

Particular premises

The seventh rule of syllogism concerns two specific premises, which cannot be followed by any conclusion.
Example

"Some mammals live in the water", "Some birds are mammals", then "Some birds live in the water".

The Pejorative

The eighth law of syllogism envisages that the conclusion always contains the pejorative part of the premises.

It is ensued that, if a premise is negative, the conclusion must also be negative, whereas if a premise is particular the conclusion must also be particular.

Example

"All dogs bark", "Some dogs are pets", then "All pets bark".

VIOLATING THE ACCEPTABILITY CRITERION

Appeal to authority

This fallacy violates the acceptability criterion and it is defined by the Latin phrase "Argomentum ab auctoritate", meaning appeal to authority.

This type of logical fallacy presumes that a proposition is deemed true because it is supported or guaranteed by an authority, or a source considered authoritative.

The appeal to authority is undoubtedly an extremely valid and legitimate, if not highly desirable method, especially in cases of scientific or medical disputes, or any other argument, which requires a deep and trustworthy knowledge of the subject matter. However, even those considered authoritative sources may fall into error and sometimes what a presumed expert is asserting might not be applicable to the argument at issue because it is irrelevant to the context or irrelevant in essence.

Example
"We must expel artists from the State because Plato said so."
"I read it in the newspapers!"

False authority

The "appeal to authority" does not concern the cases where the authoritativeness of the argument is legitimate and coherent with the context.
Unfortunately, there are cases where it is not legitimate or coherent with context, but is false instead.
The fallacy occurs when a proposition is presumed to be true despite the speaker not being authoritative and having no authority to support and validate the truthfulness of the argument.

Example
"A friend of mine, who is an architect, is vegan and he argues that veganism is the healthiest diet you can choose"
The architect friend does not have the competence or the academic titles to assert so firmly that veganism is the best diet possible.

"If the Coach had made the changes when needed, we would have not lost the match and we, as football fans would not be here losing our hearts"

Typically, post-match comments by football fans underlie a pretence of knowledgeable authority on the argument. However, such authoritativeness is not legitimized by any specific competence on their part.

Link Youtube
https://bit.ly/2sbzljm (Tom Cruise on psychology)

Appeal to emotions

The New York Times published a report in 2016[67] where it pointed out that the most engaging and attractive articles for readers were the most emotionally charged stories, or those reflecting the moods of the masses.

The role played by emotions and public involvement has become crucial in the world of information.

There are various ways to manipulate the emotional impact that news can generate on a public audience, varying in size and dependant on several contexts.

There are numerous logical fallacies and rhetorical tricks to leverage the least irrational part of the human mind. These artifices can disrupt and corrupt rational debate to a great extent.

The logical fallacies may refer to negative feelings, such as sadness, fear, hatred, shame or greed; or they may leverage positive emotions like hope, joy, happiness or safety.

---

[67] https://nyti.ms/2ktXByr

The logical fallacies based on emotions are generally characterised by one or more statements referring directly to emotions themselves, or they may relate to a specific mood of the mass. These fallacies deliberately ignore the rational debate and leverage the expected emotional response from the target public. Fake news and propaganda content work along the same lines and bet on the impact of mass emotions capable of involving and enticing the public[68].

An important MIT-conducted study[69] revealed how fake news go viral not only through the methods of disseminating the news, but primarily thanks to the emotional feature gaining advantage on the human neurological structure. By its own nature, human mind is inclined to get deeply involved with feelings, if they are triggered by the same emotional cues or signals surrounding human life.

A group of researchers created a database of words used by Twitter users in response to some fake content researchers were studying. Researchers also used a Software of "Sentiment Analysis" to process the words.

The results of their survey showed that fake news tends to have a more powerful emotional appeal when it is essentially associated with astonishment or disdain. Therefore, we see why fake news easily appeal to social network audiences. [70]

Business and politics

---

[68] https://bit.ly/2Eg5wXD

[69] https://bit.ly/2Dj5BJe

[70] https://theatln.tc/2HhAHn4

The reference to emotions, such as, hope, fear, hatred, or even national or patriotic feelings, allow any speaker to catch the public's attention and reinforce the self-identification process listeners experience during a speech.

Commercial adverts constantly refer to emotions in an attempt to connect products or brand name to positive emotions, or when, according to requirement, commercials try to establish a link with strong, resolute, exciting, encouraging or heart-warming feelings.

In 2014 the ''Institute for Psychology and Neurosciences of Glasgow University, published an essay[71] according to which, human beings only have four types of emotions to base human sensibility on: happiness, sadness, astonishment/fear and anger/disgust.

Many brand names have chosen to link up their product to pleasant emotions with reassuring content and scenes of joy.

Take the "Coca Cola" brand, which, besides boasting Santa Claus[72] as ambassador, (a symbol carrying joy in the whole of the western world) carries the slogan "Taste the feeling" in its main headlines to associate images of its product with joyful emotions.

If cleverly conceived, even messages containing cues of unhappiness can add value to a brand name or the commercial spot of an advertising promoter.

Every four years, sequels of P&G heart-breaking adverts dedicated to mothers are displayed at the start of the Olympics   Games.[73]

---

[71] https://bit.ly/2KWSn9l

[72] https://bit.ly/2gtMBOg

[73] https://bit.ly/19byNDK

Brands are not the only ones resorting to cognitive bias, or indulging in emotionalism.

In politics, the recourse to rage, hatred or fear is often a standard practice for party propaganda that aims at sending pre-packaged messages filled with prejudice or spreading unfounded fears and beliefs to hit the instincts of voters.

Many political candidates have the need to move their arguments around to pick up their electorate's moods of the moment. They often intercept and funnel the emotions and feelings of their campaigns into bias to turn popular discontent into consensus.

Moving apart from the "four basic emotions" described by the Scottish university and return to other positive feelings, we cannot help but remembering one definitely positive emotion, i.e. the "hope" of the message circulating during Obama's 2018 campaign in his famous headline "Yes we can".

President Trump did follow through with his personal slogan "Make America Great Again" which leveraged a patriotic sentiment mixed with rage for what America had turned into, because of Obama's reforms, according to Trump.

How can we not mention the European xenophobic right-wing forces who made a genuine warhorse of the alleged migrant invasion to foment racial tensions and stir up voters to increase consensus.

In the first months of 2018, Amnesty International warned that Italy was steeped in racism and a climate of hostility towards migrant because of toxic electoral campaigns, which sparked across France, Austria, Hungary and UK in the same year.

MISLEADING
MULTIMEDIA

MISLEADING GRAPHS

The ability to spread disinformation is accomplished not only with written texts, but also through fallacious graphs and data charts.

We generally tend to assume that, scientists, journalists or any expert use data and graphical charts objectively, and with the utmost transparency.

Nonetheless, in news especially, data is frequently distorted or mystified to reinforce the thesis purported by the article or propaganda message, to feed the "confirmation bias" further.[74]

A typical way to distort data in graph representations is to omit the "zero" in the abscissa value and the y-axis in a Cartesian system. [75]

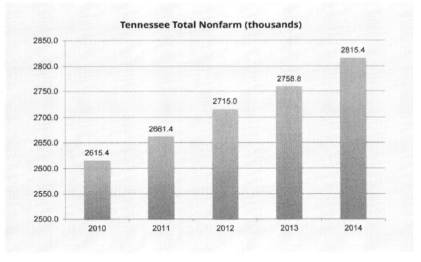

---

74 https://bit.ly/2GSYaKE
75 https://bit.ly/2satd0e

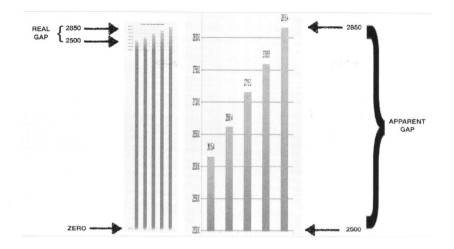

Another mystification example is found in visual graphs that refer to cumulative data.

Tracing the line of cumulative data which necessarily rises, (except in very extreme cases), makes it possible to hide degrowth, in absolute terms, given a defined time.

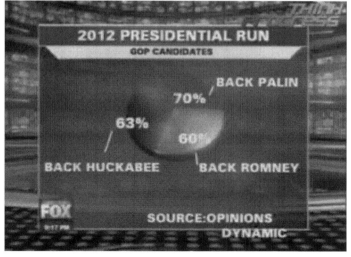

Lastly, data visualized can be distorted if standard statistical and mathematical parameters, used to set data visualization[76], are not considered.

As an example, the graph pie reported by Fox News during the 2012 Presidential primaries, displays the three slices, which do not add up to 100%, making the chart invalid.

FAKE VIDEOS

New technologies offer additional and exceptional tools to create fake multimedia content.

The development of artificial intelligence, artificial neural networks and automated machine-learning equipment have enabled developers to devise software, which were totally unthinkable ten years ago.

 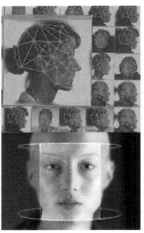

---

[76] https://read.bi/2sdoyKM

Recent developments in the field of Artificial Intelligence have proven it is possible to recreate a lip-sync video from an audio input which perfectly imitates the person in the act of uttering the video words.

Washington University researchers conceived a fake video of Obama by using a radio input, and an obvious forgery too, where they used the "machine learning" software to lip-sync the words Obama would say. They achieved a realistic video of Obama where he spoke the words of the fake audio message[77].

Researchers analysed more than 140 hours of Obama's speeches and videos to develop the model to create the clone video of Obama.

Similar examples of video manipulation through "machine learning" have happened in Europe too.

In Germany, for example, some young developers took great amusement in manipulating Putin's face, expressions and grimaces to set up fake videos similar to the Obama model.

---

[77] https://bit.ly/2oCKUWL

This type of multimedia fake content created with "machine learning" technologies is called "DeepFake".

"Revenge porn" is one of them, for instance.

Other types of software like FakeApp, which uses Google "Tensorflow" technology, allow face change or face replacement during the video editing.

In theory, anyone can take any adult-only video, manipulate it with high quality images or pictures and make target person appear in the video.

Famous Hollywood actress, Emma Watson, ended up in various pornographic websites with her face craftily attached to the body of an adult movie performer.

In many cases, social networks or streaming-video platforms, like Youtube, help these fake videos go viral quickly, with a hundred million people visualizing them and often giving rise to fake news originated from counterfeit video.

In 2016, Woolshed Company, a small independent movie producer located in Melbourne,[78] admitted to be responsible for the creation and dissemination of some of the most celebrated fake videos in the web.

To quote some notorious titles of fake videos distributed by Woolshed: "A man fights a white shark", "A girl is almost struck by a lightning", "A man chases a tornado in the outback to shoot a selfie", "Snowboarder unknowingly trailed by a bear", and many more[79].

These videos are originated as entertainment to attract the highest number of visualizations possible.

When a news editor decides to report the fake video news, in turn, he is generating further fake news. It is self-evident that most of the time news is nonsensical and its peculiar features of "absurdness" or "incredibility" are a major factor in attracting people to the video. These features greatly contribute to the video virality or the video association with a clickbait title.

Video manipulation may also be used with cynical, malicious, macabre or sinister purpose.

Fake videos are not immune to the influence exerted by politics or the needs required by electoral campaigns. For example, among the most viral videos of 2017, there was one showing an Afro-American little girl who pointed fingers at President Trump and addressed him as "a disgrace to the world".

---

[78] https://dailym.ai/29KC02o

[79] https://bit.ly/2LAundc

The video was visualized more than 12 million times and shared or re-tweeted 250 thousand times, receiving almost half a million interactions[80].

Trump was impersonated by an actor, Tony Atamanuik, during the "Comedy Central President's Show".

FAKE AUDIOS

Artificial intelligence algorithms are capable of re-processing audio frequencies, in addition to images and videos. A team of researchers of Chinese giant tech company "Baidu" developed a project to explore the borders of neural networks and artificial intelligence applied to sound and audio cloning, namely, Deep Voice[81]. The study analyses different samples of feminine and masculine voices. They are subsequently processed by algorithms which formulate a clone audio track[82].

The more samples the algorithm can process, the closest/or most faithful the clone audio track is.[83]

Initially, this software needed at least 20 minutes for each sample to clone the track.

At present, the software is able to reproduce a verisimilar audio track by analysing any sample audio, as source, in just   3.7   seconds.

---

[80] https://bit.ly/2w8GFVj
[81] https://bit.ly/2GUGr5w
[82] https://bit.ly/2GvGhBP
[83] https://audiodemos.github.io/

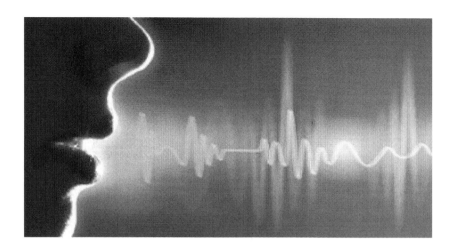

The chapter of artificial intelligence applied to sound rendering from a brief voice sample is extremely interesting.

It is a concrete possibility to innovate communication systems speeding up the audio recognition process, besides content mystification and distribution, which it is safe to guard against anyway.

In 2016 Adobe introduced its new software "VoCo", able to generate a clone audio with a time of analysis of 20 minutes from original sample.

In addition, Lyrebir, a startup based in Montreal, claims to be able to get a clone audio from a single minute of original audio sample.

Likewise, the technologies behind fake videos could help us send or receive audio messages in the future.

Those audio messages could automatically be transformed into videos.

DEBUNKING

Admittedly, the battle to combat fake news is not easy at all, especially if we consider the world of Fake News in its entirety, that is to say, the huge media impact that propaganda and fallacious information play on public opinion.

There are now various processes, which can prevent, in some cases, or deconstruct, in others, fallacious news.

In journalism, and, more generally speaking, in the news industry, standard practice for news desk should be to verify news content before publication. This procedure called verification refers to all standard practices used by editorial staff to check the accuracy and reliability of a statement, a reported quote or any data used.

"The Elements of Journalism" is a book authored by Tom Resenstiel and Bill Kovack, who argue that the function of checking facts and verifying information constitutes the real and true essence of journalism.

The process known as "verification" is detailed as an almost scientific discipline aimed at collecting facts with the obligation of truth.

Tom Resenstiel and Bill Kovack

Unfortunately, we have had experiences contrary to these principles, and in many instances, the function to verify facts and sources, or themes purported in news articles, is regrettably neglected, for various reasons.

Hence, we are inundated with flows of unchecked fallacious news and fake information, on a daily basis.

The public audience could actively enter the game and take steps to question the veracity of news, and by using its critic judgement, attempt to deconstruct, and where required, debunk fake news or fallacious content.

As previously mentioned, this process is called "Debunking" where the term signifies "remove the bunk";

i.e. the prefix "de" means to take away and the word "bunk" means nonsense.

The introduction of this term in his modern usage first appeared in 1923, when American novel writer, William E.Woodward published his bestseller called "Bunk".

Then, the word debunking became widespread in its current meaning and assumed the meaning of "take the bunks out of things", or "remove nonsense from things".

A debunker is the person who zealously practices the activity of exposing or demystifying pseudo-scientific theories, hoaxes and any fake, dubious and pretentious news, with the aid of scientific methodologies. [84]

---

[84] «To expose or ridicule the falseness, sham, or exaggerated claims of». *Debunker - American Heritage Dictionary of the English Language.*

Until late 20th century, debunkers like Philip Klass used to study UFO phenomena, fanciful appearances or supernatural events.
Today, debunkers deals primarily with fake news and have gained an unusual prominence in the news and information industry.

Nowadays, university associations and research centres alike are very keen on promoting new initiatives to debunk fake news. The National Institute of Standards and Technology debunked the world-famous conspiracy theory that alleged Twin Towers had been pulled down in a controlled explosion.

A very successful practice in debunking news specifically related to journalism, and currently widely diffused, is Fact Checking.
Fact checker is a word coined by American journalism in the 20's of 1900 and it refers to the person who verifies any given statement or news, and the reliability of

information by sourcing experts and government agencies.

There are currently more than 50 worldwide associations, institutions and centres operating in the field of fact checking.

In 2016, a news reporter, Federica Cherubini, stressed the constant growth of Fact-Checking websites in Europe, from Ireland to Turkey.

Over the last 5 years, debunking and verification techniques have proven to be pivotal in the existence of information, and caused an increasing interest by industry pundits.

CONTENT VERIFICATION

To contrast the phenomenon of Fake News following a few basic rules can help avoiding being caught in their trap.

The bulk of fake news is disseminated through digital media and, with that in mind, it is good advice to avail the opinion of the many experts found in the web, whether journalists, scientists, debunkers, or other reliable and authoritative professional associations to verify digital or traditional media news.

A comparison of news read versus the analysis performed by fact-checker websites is a prerequisite to correct use and learning of modern information.

Among the most distinguished fact-checking websites, we suggest PolitiFact.com, a project sponsored by the St.

Petersburg Times, which conducts activities of debunking and fact checking with reference to American politics.

We also indicate Snopes.com, one of the most reliable online source to fight hoaxes and fake news, founded and directed by Barbara and David P. Mikkelson, who set up the website in 1995.

Slayer.com is another website against email frauds, scams and hoaxes in general. The website also offers its users tutorial content to improve online security.

A further website founded in 1999, called Fiction.org, provides users with a "reality checking" service through email.

In the event you might not be able to use a fact checker website, our advice is to always carry out some standard procedures to verify news accuracy and reliability, whether it is online content, current event or a piece of information.

First and foremost, you need to check the news source, which, in case of digital media, can be easily verified starting from its URL address[85].

---

[85] Uniform Resource Locator, is a sequel of characters, which

In cases of online articles, checking the publication date can help finding out if news is current, or just a refrain to exacerbate the debate.

Browsing any links (if present) related to the article is also a good practice to verify source reliability and destination, that is, links aiming at spurious and mystified claims.

Finally, do a quick exam of the "keywords and sentences" found in the article, since an overinflated, exaggerated, offensive or sectarian claim is often evidence of a dubious and suspicious article.

In addition, we recommend investigating data or graph chart accuracy and reliability because they are frequently distorted to support the purported fact or news.

---

unequivocally identify the address of an Internet resource, such as a document or an image

VISUAL VERIFICATION

Images and videos plays a fundamental role in modern information.

Analysts expect more than 80% of online traffic will come from visual content [86] in the next few years.

The volume of visual content has currently reached figures deemed unimaginable until a few years ago.

At present, Facebook Messenger users share approximately 216 thousand images every minute, and to that volume, roughly 2 billion Instagram likes must add.

In the case of Youtube, the ultimate video platform every minute corresponds to 400 hours of new videos loaded[87].

News information is no exception, of course, and like similar industries, it has witnessed the constant rise of the visual world.

Indeed, visual images have taken the lead in the distribution of news and information, although image and video manipulation started long before the digital era.

We mention the first case of image manipulation dating back to 1860 when a portrait of President Abraham Lincoln was retouched and his face was ''copied/pasted to the body of the seated protagonist of a famous painting by Mathew Brady.

---

[86] https://bit.ly/2eV64tp

[87] https://bit.ly/2xfxTqp - Digital Year Review (2016)

Abraham Lincoln

The portrait of the two images stitched together as one was used for printing the US five-dollar banknote.

Other well-known image manipulations were done by dictatorships in the second half of the 20th century. Another piece of art trickery was the picture of Stalin portrayed with agent Nikolai Yezhov, later removed by altering the image.

Stalin and Yezhov

Video and image manipulation has reached outstanding levels in our digital era, thanks to programs like Adobe Photoshop or Blender.

We cannot emphasize strongly enough how necessary it has become to adopt a good verification practice of visual content as well as text. Most fallacious or propagandistic news pass through visual content. The image copyright must always be visible and failing to do so, might imply image could have been used without authorisation, or the subject person be false. Hence a presumed image alteration.

The copyright allows you to trace image and where there is no Photo-credit found, Google comes to rescue with a 'reverse image search' option.

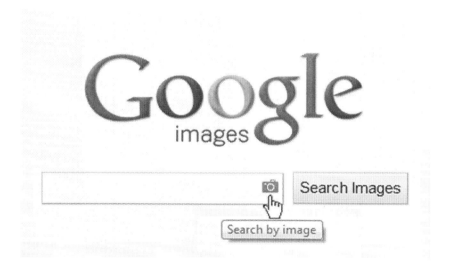

The same rules we applied to text work for images. To check date and place where image was created, for example, and the fact that showed odd, nonsensical or abnormal situations should point to the dubious veracity of the image itself.

Additionally, it may help to become acquainted with EXIF image files data since this data is normally stored in a jpeg file, and it indicates date when image was shot and type of camera used.

The feature set up by Jeffrey Friedl and called EXIF Viewer, facilitates image data retrieval and even image localisation on a map through a smartphone or any geolocalized device.

We must duly and unfortunately note that EXIF data is often lost when images are loaded in Internet websites or social media, or also when modified with Photoshop.

EXIF Information			
File name:	DSC_0260.JPG	File size:	922866 bytes
File date:	2006:04:22 22:06:16	Camera make:	NIKON CORPORATION
Camera model:	NIKON D70s	Date/Time:	2006:04:17 18:06:08
Resolution:	3000 x 2632	Flash used:	No
Focal length:	18.0mm (35mm equivalent: 27mm)	Exposure time:	0.0008 s (1/1250)
Aperture:	f/8.0	Whitebalance:	Manual
Metering Mode:	matrix	Exposure:	Manual
Exposure Mode:	ManualAuto bracketing		

There are various software and web services if you need to check and authenticate the image truthfulness, accuracy and reliability, such as, Izitru.com.

You can verify if an image has been altered (or jargon word is photoshopped"), by using web services like fotoForensics.com. This tool enables users to find out if an image was manipulated with editing software.

217

As for videos, you can follow the same advice given for content and images, i.e. check the URL address and internal links within the video, question the image credibility if over the top, verify origin and quality of shots etc. etc.

Google also offers a Plugin for Google Chrome to check video source, a tool developed and promoted by European project "InVid". Amnesty International has also developed an online help tool with support of YouTube, which can be used to check the video URL.[88]

SOCIAL MEDIA VERIFICATION

It is not at all easy to reach users and spread true news. Despite efforts on the part of associations and institutions to publish objective content to contrast fake news and propaganda, it is not infrequent that the same analysis originate from reference sites used.

As repeatedly said in the course of this book, social media, namely Facebook and Twitter, have gained a central role in the distribution of fake and fallacious news.

Therefore, it is of primary importance for those involved with news information, to know the exact mechanisms of social media verification; be capable of performing activities of monitoring and verification of social media themselves; analyse the media events interaction with social content flows.

---

[88] https://bit.ly/2J7EfNw

Social media trends can tell a lot on the impact a specific media event is having in the digital audience or the lifespan of a news.

Tools like Hootsuite, Google Trends and Twitter Trends can contribute to monitor hot trend topics on Social Networks.

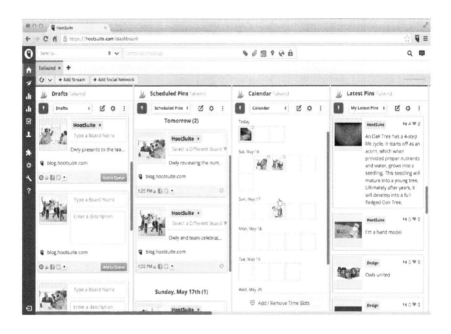

The monitoring of hot trends has pointed out that user attention in Social Networks is extremely volatile.
Users tend to dwell on a content superficially, and for only a short lap, browsing from one content to the other. The attention of users surfing the web is conceptually very rushed and hasty.

219

It often happens that users come across news, which is not intrinsically fallacious, but bound to become misleading when social network users interact with it.

Various studies have already shown that 70% of Facebook comments, shares or interactions with an article without reading it, or reading just the title.

The consequence might sometimes conduct to a misunderstanding between the editor's intention and the public's reaction in social media.

By paradox, the public's reaction is conditioned not much by content, but response from other users. Some fallacious content often comes from an automated machine devised to inflate results or vanity metrics of comments, likes, shares or retweets.

We have previously mentioned how, during the 2016 Presidential campaign, several agencies connected to the Republican Party started off a spate of bots and fake accounts to launch propaganda messages on behalf of political party agencies.

This leads us to another focal point related to fake news, that is, to check not only that the content is genuinely true, but also that social media profiles of those reporting or sharing the content, are reliable.

In case of private citizen sharing news it is advisable to check how frequently they publish, the depth of topics, the origin or source, the ratio between active and passive connections (following versus follower).

For public pages, for example, associations or institutions, it is important to trace down the real page administrator or person responsible for page content.

TOOLS

In recent years, greater attention has been focused on projects that develop tools capable of helping users to verify and question news content, and be guided through the ocean of news in online information.

We hereby include a short list of some web services, which might be useful when you carry out your own personal search, or other activities of Debunking, Fact Checking and Visual Verification.

Snopes.com

Snopes.com[89] was one of first internet websites specifically dedicated to Fact-Checking and is considered the reference web page to debunk Urban Legends.

Founded in 1994 by David and Barbara Mikkelson, today, snopes.com is reported as source of information by important traditional media like CNN, MSNBC, Fortune, Forbes and The New York Times.
In March 2009, the website had more than 6 million visits a month, because of the large volume of articles debunking hoaxes or fake news.

---

89 https://www.snopes.com/

PolitiFact

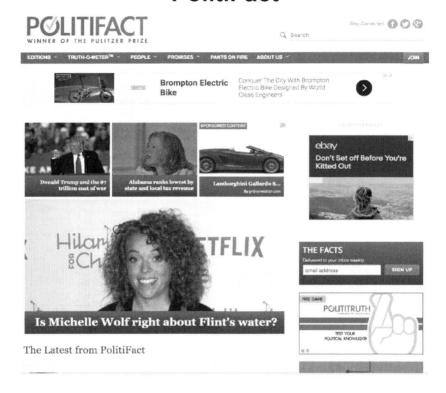

The Latest from PolitiFact

PolitiFact was launched in 2007 as an editorial project of the Tampa Bay Times, (later called St. Petersburg Times), and it is the largest newspaper in Florida, mostly concerned with US politics.

It is merely a newspaper initiative focused on activities to debunk current events, or political and news statements. Very similar to snopes.com, PolitiFact is a fact-checking website which provides factual analysis or objective investigations of political statements, propagandistic messages or related misleading data.

Project InVid

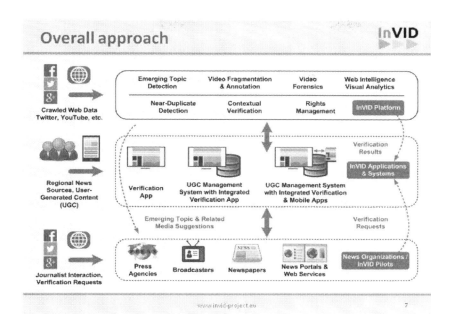

InVid is a vast-scale project,[90] which should be launched in the second half of 2018 and be financed by Horizon 2020 funds.

The project includes a platform, which offers services to identify, refute and report fake news and fake content.

An ad hoc Plugin will be available for Chrome and Firefox to report fake news and verify image and video origin and reliability.

---

[90] https://bit.ly/2y2vSNt

Reverse Search Image

Google, the giant tech company with headquarters in Mountain View, CA, has also decided to provide users with tools to combat fake content, or at least, verify image origin.

The "reverse image search[91] service is now available for mobile devices and it allows users to upload an image and trace its page of origin, or the image metadata if they can be located by Google search engines.

TinyEye[92] is another service tool that allows to perform the "reverse image search" to even verify when and where the searched image was previously used.

---

[91] https://reverse.photos/
[92] https://tineye.com/

Fact Checking Tag

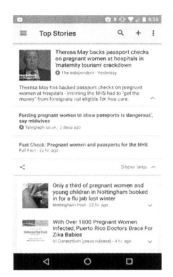 

Clearly, Google's commitment to fight back fake news is evident from the introduction of the recent "Fact Checking" tag.

Towards the end of 2017, Google has begun introducing the new tag in all countries where it is present. This feature will allow users to identify fact-checking articles before potentially fake news articles. The marked introduction of the Fact-Checking Tag found in SERP (acronym for search engine results page) should enable users to select valid and reliable content.

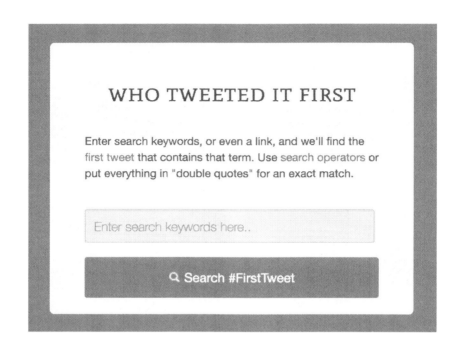

Ctrlq.org/first

This tool[93] was developed by Amit Agarwal, a computer and software engineer who founded Labnol[94]. The tool can identify the first Tweet containing a given hashtag or search keyword and, consequently, it is very useful to trace back the origin of viral events in social media, often concocted through botnets, false profiles and false influencers. Using the toll makes it viable to track down the first Tweet that originated initial retweets,

---

[93] http://ctrlq.org/first/

[94] https://www.labnol.org/

commentaries and replies and, most importantly, carry out a specific analysis on the credibility, one-sidedness and authoritativeness of person who first started the virality chain.

PIZZAGATE — FIRST TWEET

THE FIRST MENTION OF PIZZAGATE ON TWITTER WAS MADE BY @PROCESS_X

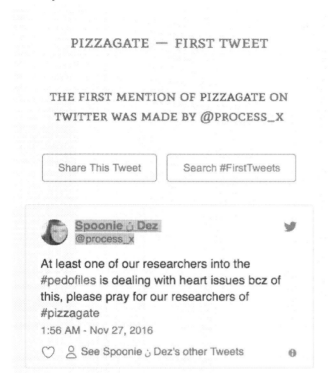

Share This Tweet   Search #FirstTweets

Spoonie ⚶ Dez
@process_x

At least one of our researchers into the #pedofiles is dealing with heart issues bcz of this, please pray for our researchers of #pizzagate

1:56 AM - Nov 27, 2016

♡ See Spoonie ⚶ Dez's other Tweets

228

Twazzup

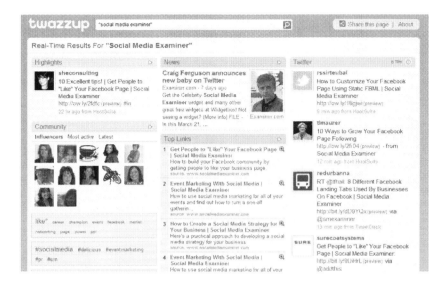

There is a further tool to monitor Twitter-based activities within the field of social media verification, This tool[95] allows to trace back the network of people who send 'tweets' on a specific argument by selection of a given hashtag or search keyword.

Twazzup collects the most popular Tweets and the people who made the topic a hot trend, thus tracing influencers or other profiles who are interacting or have interacted with search keyword under scrutiny.

Amnesty Youtube DataViewer

---

[95] http://new.twazzup.com/

Youtube DataViewer

https://www.youtube.com/watch?v=7R-V02MS

Russian army in Syria

Russian army training in the port of the city of Tartus, Syria where located Russian naval base FACEBOOK: https://www.facebook.com/FuerzaMilitar SUBSCRIBE: http://www.youtube.com/c/FuerzasArmadasTV Fuerzas Armadas™ 2015 About the video / Community guidelines: This footage is NOT intended to be violent, shocking, sensational, disrespectful or glorify violence in any way. We are sharing this footage STRICTLY for the purposes of news reporting, educating and documentating. Fuerzas Armadas is a news channel where we strive to show people the news that has been left out of the main-stream media. This footage is also part of an ongoing documentary on 'events that shape our perspective'.

Video ID: 7R-V02MSQvA
Upload Date (YYYY/MM/DD): 2015-09-12
Upload Time (UTC): 00:37:09 (convert to local time)

This tool,[96] developed and sponsored by Amnesty International, has enabled users to analyse and extract information of Youtube videos based on its specific URL.

DataViewer will supply Thumbnails (the video preview image), in addition to other relevant information related to video origin and date of creation; this information being important in Google reverse search image.

---

[96] https://bit.ly/2rVWWuW

FotoForensic

The above-mentioned tool[97] allows one to verify image origin and authenticity, even in cases of counterfeit, photoshopping or other image editing.

97 http://fotoforensics.com/

POSSIBLE SOLUTIONS

ARTIFICIAL INTELLIGENCE

Artificial intelligence is among the possible solutions to adopt to stem the tide of fake news.

Several developers in the world are actually in the process of implementing adequate tools to detect false news from reliable stories worthy of our trust and attention.

There are a number of Newcos and Startups, which are currently trying to develop artificial-intelligence based solutions to help us_identify or discerning reliable news from fake.

One of these companies engaged in the development of an artificial intelligence solution, AdVerif.ai, in November 2017,[98] published an algorithm, which can identify corrupted content or distorted news with 90% accuracy, according to the company offering the service.

---

[98] https://bit.ly/2j0U8qf

Major brands such as Adidas or Nike, from North Europe to North America are financing research and development of this algorithm.

The algorithm[99] has been "trained" to automatically study and learn all subtle differences found in reliable and unreliable news content.
Thanks to a series of fake, mystified, incorrect news and information the **AdVerif.ai** algorithm can recognise from the basic web structure notions and the source verification to even the more technical aspects of language used, for example, a propensity for excessive and incorrect adverbs or the flawed sentence syntaxes

A better performance of this algorithm could be ensured if it could interact with a "commonly-shared information" database. The access to further objective and factual reference data would increase to a minimum the algorithm scope of action therefore reducing the error margin produced by antinomies, misinterpretations or dubious semantic understanding.
The implementation of NLP (Natural Language Processing) technologies and the conjoined use of public or Open Source database, such as, Wikipedia and its Linked Data project, will allow algorithms to access a more and more "human" knowledge. This would give enormous support to information analysis.

---

[99] http://adverifai.com/

BLOCKCHAIN

Another recent technology that looks reliably promising in fighting fake news is Blockchain, literally meaning "chain to block". This technology is a process where more than one subject share computer resources such as memory, CPU, Band, Data etc. etc.

The end purpose is to give users a virtual database, either public or private, where every participant owns an unchangeable set of data.

Using an automatically updated protocol, considered safe by the user community, in conjunction with encrypted validation techniques originate mutual trust among participants, compared to data stored by Blockchain.

Metaphorically speaking, we could say that a blockchain represents a huge and shared "register" which monitors data within the same blockchain, and also guarantees that all chain participants are trustworthy, in the same way banks, insurers and editors do with the use of a unique ISBN code for each customer.

In addition, if Blockchain was applied to the world of information, would guarantee a system of meritocratic trust where media publishing quality information would be rewarded. On the contrary, media not complying with standards of adequate and correct information (fake newsmakers) could be punished, fined, sabotaged, or even expelled from the news networking.

Blockchain could be used in the same way to act like a technologic safeguard of all that concerns digital sources making news: images, videos and content of social media accounts.

In November 2017, an international project named "Publiq"[100] was published with the intent to be the first media distribution system to use Blockchain technology or other artificial intelligence systems to guarantee an ecosystem of quality and valuable information.

BLOCKCHAIN
DISTRIBUTED MEDIA

INTERNATIONAL COMMITTEE

In the last five years, rumours have spread about the creation of a supposed international committee to combat fake news and disinformation.

Among the possible solutions to fight fake news, it has been suggested that an impartial and supranational agency could be set up to perform the monitoring of media environments in all countries, and report any abuse, distortions or violations of factual reality.
In Europe, the EJO (European Journalism Observatory) has dedicated a section of its website to the topic of fake

---

[100] https://bit.ly/2GTsepJ

news in America and the European Commission itself has filed an investigation on the subject.

In early 2018, US Congress summoned Mark Zuckerberg to question Facebook responsibility in spreading targeted fake content through the London firm, Cambridge Analytica.

One could express some scepticism as for the current position of the European Commission towards Mark Zuckerberg. Indeed, a few years earlier, the man himself had suggested the creation of an impartial committee of journalists. The idea would have been to improve Facebook News Feed, however such proposed idea never follow suit.

The constitution of a committee made of communication experts, or journalists and information pundits is as fascinating as undoubtedly very complex to realise.

The stakes or vested interest of all countries, and in turn of businesses and political parties, make the universe of information extremely liable to use of subjective opinions and prone to relativism.

In spite of its expected complexity, various institutions, associations and research centres focus constantly on the issue of fake news and propaganda. Indeed, the ball has long been in the court of international politics.

Nonetheless, the role of an international agency for the spreading of correct information is as complicated as desirable.

NEWS LITERACY PROGRAM

All tools are really effective if supported by a critical and wise   reasoning.

The most effective solutions to fight the plague of fake news would most likely be the education and awareness of single individuals and the collective public opinion.

Nations and institutions should encourage the formation of a greater critical consciousness to fight one-sided and sectarian news and propaganda. A same educational role is desirable on the part of all entities involved with knowledge, culture and sense of judgement so that positive results could be seen in the medium-long run.
Associations, institutions and research centres have already started moving in the direction of providing technological and academic tools apt to deal with this recent way to use information.
One of the pioneering institutions in the education industry of correct information is "News Literacy Project", an American association which, already in 2009, had launched an educational program called "Checkology", aimed at teaching primary school children how to distinguish facts from fiction.

We will be able to fight back the alarming threat of fake news and information, or current mass-manipulation, only by educating new generations to find their way through the maze of an increasingly information-focused world.

CASE HISTORY

The Pizzagate Conspiracy

During the 2016 US electoral campaign, hackers broke the personal email account of John Podesta, Campaign Manager of Hillary Clinton. The fake news originated by hackers construed a string of emails which contained coded messages referring to paedophilia and human trafficking, and involving several restaurants and high-ranking officials of the Democratic Party.

The headquarters of such activity being the pizza place called "Comet Ping Pong" in Washington.

The launch of the conspiracy first began in 8chan and 4chan, to be later spread by pro-Trump websites, reaching Facebook, Reddit and Twitter, even causing a shooting at the hand of a conspiracy fanatic.

The cost of UE

All along the Brexit referendum campaign, 'Vote Leave' supporters circulated the news that the European Union was costing roughly £350m a week, that is to say, £20bn a year. Leave campaigners claimed that these resources could be better used to fund the national health system (NHS).

Although United Kingdom sends EU more money than what it receives through financing, funds and benefits, figures are rather different.

UK yearly contributions were indeed £8.5bn, therefore, £160m a week. This amount accounted for less than half of what declared by 'Vote Leave' Campaigners.

The fake news had long been a widespread pet subject of the campaign and largely diffused on TV, radio, newspapers and Webzines.

Google buys Apple!

The fake news came from the very Dow Jones News Feed in the autumn of 2017.

Fake News purported that Google had bought Apple for $9bn, but the fake news lifespan was very short. Once debunked, the news was quick to disappear, but the time it lingered on, was long enough for automatic bots to start purchasing Apple stock, and generate a real rise in its stock value.

Hurricane Irma

Hurricane Irma hit the Caribbean in September 2017 and wreaked havoc on a scale never seen before.

However, a great portion of online information and viral videos shared in social networks, were largely false. Old footage and false videos circulated in social media for weeks on end, though relating to previous hurricanes.

It proved difficult to tell hoaxes from inaccuracies, and some content visualizations skyrocketed insomuch that official news channels had to reassure and advise readers to check information before getting alarmed.

Some posts classified hurricane Irma as category 6 when all existing sources placed it under category 5.

Dan Scavino, the White House Head for Social Media, fell for the fake news too and shared a picture of Miami airport being flooded. He was quickly disproved by the same airport staff who pointed out the shared picture did not even represent Miami airport.

Palm oil

In recent years, media have launched a really fierce

attack against palm oil. Accused to harm health greatly and being carcinogenic, be a big pollutant because its farming was destroying forests, palm oil was removed by major food and cosmetics companies from almost any product. The industry quickly proclaimed from the rooftops that palm oil was no longer being used.

Media conducted campaigns to inform public of palm oil alleged harmfulness, in addition to a massive online propaganda and no palm oil tags in every product package. However, the news was totally unsubstantiated.

A little bit of search using scientific and established sources of information would have proved that, among all alternative oils, palm oil is the healthiest, most cost-effective and environmentally sustainable.

Briefly, palm oil is as detrimental to health as butter, and, hence, not harmful if used moderately. Rather, it is by far the least hazardous fat in a scale of chemically treated oils.

Immigrants

An hilarious case broke out in the summer of 2017, when actor Samuel L. Jackson and NBA basket player, Magic

Johnson, shared pictures in which they flaunted Prada, Louis Vuitton and other expensive bags, during a shopping frenzy in Forte dei Marmi, Italy.

Italian satirist and journalist Luca Bottura used the picture for one of his memes to conduct a social experiment.
The claim alleged that these two immigrants were using the so-called "benefit" of €35, granted by government for personal expenses.
The *meme* in question clearly became viral, and despite the blatantly ironical and mocking tone, the numerous commentaries and shares to the Post showed how many had baited the hook.
Hence, test accomplished!

Earvin Magic Johnson @ @MagicJohnson · 16 ago

Sam & I chilling out on a bench yesterday in Forte dei Marmi, Italy. The fans started lining up to take pictures with us.

Oprah and Weinstein

Following the unfolding of Weinstein scandal, many women came forward in support of others who had suffered or were still suffering domestic violence.

Oprah Winfrey was among them, and her opening speech at the Golden Globes Awards began with mention of women's rights to fight harassment and the call to arms of all women facing abuse.

Winfrey was highly criticised because her closeness to Weinstein was well documented and many thought that she knew of his misconduct and accepted.
The news that circulated virally as online meme is undoubtedly false though, and Oprah Winfrey never introduced young women to Weinstein to satisfy his sexual appetite.

The Withdrawal of Big Mac

The most celebrated fast-food club sandwich, featuring in every menu of McDonald restaurants was taken out. Why did McDonald withdraw the flagship product? Easier said than done! The news is false.

The hoax is initially spread by a well-known fake news website whose name "abcnews-us.com" can be confused with the existing ABC News, a trusted source of news and information.
The news is shared and believed to be true by thousand users in social networks despite it had been originated by highly unreliable sources.

Obama born in Kenya

During the 2008 US presidential election campaign, a spate of conspiracy theories on the ineligibility of Barack Obama invaded news.
Rumours were circulating on Barack Obama's ineligibility and supposedly not having US citizenship, as required by Article 2 of Constitution.

His birth certificate was alleged to be false and that Obama was born in Kenya and not Hawaii. Other theories alleged that Obama had taken Indonesian citizenship and therefore losing US citizenship.

These theories escalated to such a point that Obama was forced to produce an extract of his birth certificate in 2008, and again in 2011 the official, certified papers supplied by the Ministry of Health of Hawaii.
In the end, though the news was completely unfounded, it keeps coming back here and there and remain fashionable in the news.

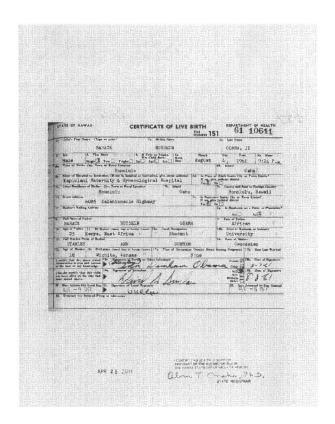

Images of Syria

Recently, and as if the situation was not bad enough, fake content has even targeted the Syrian war.
There are countless new tools to manipulate public opinion, namely the deceitful use of pictures.

Hundred and hundred Tweets or Facebook Posts are shared thousands times, although content and images might come from other wars or conflicts.

Even pictures used to substantiate posts, although true, belong to other warzones or past conflicts.
Some images were even found to be taken from

Halloween photo shootings, or were just videoclips and works of art.

A search using "Google images" can quickly help to find the way out of the maze of endless fake pictures which are published daily.

The staged murder of Babchenko

In May 2018, the Ukraine's security service staged the fake murder of Russian journalist,
Arkady Babchenko, a sworn enemy of the Kremlin, who had left Moscow in autumn, out of fear that his life was under serious threat. The Ukrainian police claimed the (fake death) set up had been necessary to disrupt the plot of Russian agents who were on the lookout for the journalist.

The story was widely reported by media around the world and confirmed by the Ukrainian government and the police, who circulated a picture of Babchenko being shot in the back three times and his body found in a pool of blood on the floor of his apartment.

The story looked plausible because Babchenko had received real threats and his fierce opposition to President Vladimir Putin was well known.
Sherlock Holmes had used the same trick triumphantly too, in order to carry out a successful investigation on a complex and intricate case.

Hence, the propagation of fake news is now an issue that calls for some serious thinking, especially if the same journalists deliberately generate forged news.

Fake News can kill

Two men lynched after WhatsApp messages wrongly claimed they were child snatchers... as chilling new trend sweeps India
The victims were beaten to death after they stopped at a village to ask for directions

Both had gone to a picnic spot in the area to visit a waterfall and were viciously attacked on their return by a mob that accused them of being "child lifters".
Earlier, rumours had circulated that two men had kidnapped a child and fled in a black car, according to local media reports.

People not only did the attackers film one of them begging for mercy but also posted them on Facebook, claiming responsibility for the murders.

They were kicked beaten by the mob with bamboo sticks and hanged from a nearby tree

Police have arrested 16 people in connection with the killings in Panjuri Kachari, in the north–eastern state of Assam.

BIBLIOGRAPHY

Russ Kick (2002), Everything You Know Is Wrong: The Disinformation Guide to Secrets and Lies

Arendt H. (1968), "Truth in politics", in Between Past and Future. Eight Exercises in Political Thought, New York, Viking Press. Arendt H. (1972), "Lying in Politics", in Crises of the Republic, New York, Harvest Books.

Perelman C. and Olbrechts-Tyteca L. (1971), The New Rhetoric. A Treatise on Argumentation, Notre Dame, University of Notre Dame Press.

Wardle C. (2017), "Fake News? It's complicated", First Draft, https://firstdraftnews.com/fake-news-complicated/ (Last consulted on 6 Sep 2017).

Marc Bloch: Memoirs of War, 1914-15 - 1989 by Cambridge University Press

Essentials of Business Communication - by Mary Ellen Guffey

Mark Kramer, Telling True Stories: A Nonfiction Writers' Guide from the Nieman Foundation at Harvard University

John R. Bender, Writing and Reporting for the Media

Daniel Levitin, Weaponized Lies: How to Think Critically in the Post-Truth Era.

Other books from the same author

FINANCIAL TIMES

Impresa 4.0

Marketing e comunicazione digitale a 4 direzioni

Franco Giacomazzi - Marco Camisani Calzolari

FT Prentice Hall

Publisher: Pearson / Financial Times
Authors: Marco Camisani Calzolari
and Franco Giacomazzi

Escape from Facebook: The Back Home Strategy
Author: Marco Camisani Calzolari

Il mondo digitale. Facile per tutti
Publisher: Mondadori
Author: Marco Camisani Calzolari

Pronto soccorso digitale per le aziende: 80 schede per sapere cosa serve davvero per sopravvivere alla rivoluzione digitale.
Publisher: HOEPLI
Author: Marco Camisani Calzolari

Author biography

Marco has been involved with the Digital industry since 1994, namely, as University Contract Professor in Digital Communication & Transformation and Fake News, in addition to being a prominent Keynote Speaker and Writer on the subject. Originally born in Milan, Marco, a well-known media personality, now lives in London and has become a British citizen. Marco is also been Digital Advisor for important multinationals such as Henkel, Roche, Atlantia, Danieli and so forth. As a Digital book writer, he has authored several publications on Digital Strategy and he is a regular contributor to many magazines inherent to digital-related topics, as well as various national TV and Radio channels where he is a long-established name, always hosted not only for his distinct competence but also great popularity with the public.

DIGITAL COMMUNICATION ADVISOR

ATLANTIA - Digital Transformation advisor (2016 to 2018)
Atlantia Spa (Holding for Autostrade per L'Italia, Aeroporti di Roma, Telepass, Revenue €3.750 billion)

DANIELI - Digital Communication advisor (2016 to 2017)
Danieli Spa (a multinational company ranks among the three largest suppliers of equipment and plants to the metal industry in the world. Revenue €2,508 billion)

ROCHE - Digital Communication and Digital Transformation advisor (2016)
Roche (Basel, Switzerland, one of the largest pharmaceutical companies in the world. Revenue 47.462 billion CHF)

MONDELEZ - KRAFT - Digital Communication and Digital Transformation advisor (2013)
Mondelez (American multinational confectionery, food, and beverage company. Revenue $25.920 billion)

HENKEL - Digital Communication and Digital Transformation advisor (2012)
Henkel (chemical and consumer goods company. Revenue €18.089 billion)

UK TI - UK TRADE AND INVESTMENT - Mentor (UK Government department)

Politics and Institutions about Communication, Propaganda, fake news and Post Truth (2004 to now) under non disclosure agreement

UNIVERSITY PROFESSOR

EUROPEAN UNIVERSITY OF ROME - Contract Professor and chair of the course in Digital Communication and Fake News (2017 to now) • Teach the course on "Fake news".
https://unier.esse3.cineca.it/Guide/PaginaADContest.do;jsessionid=0
9742798EEBECB7F13A1C218C889BABD.esse3-unier-prod-
02?ad_cont_id=10103*1219*2017*2014*9999&ANNO_ACCADEMIC
O=2017&ANNO_COORTE=2016&ANNO_REVISIONE=201

LECTURE ABOUT FAKE NEWS at LSE London School of Economics (6th February 2018)
• TLecture about "Fake news".
https://www.youtube.com/watch?time_continue=1&v=nAvQT_gMnHI

UNIVERSITY OF HAWAII - HONOLULU - Guest Lecturer in Digital Communication and Fake News (2017)
• Teach the seminar on "Fake news".
https://www.hawaii.edu/calendar/manoa/2017/08/22/31500.html?et_i
d=41462

UNIVERSITY OF PAVIA - Contract Professor and chair of the course in Business Digital Communication (2016 to now)

- Teach the course on "Business Digital Communication".
http://cim.unipv.eu/2016/10/05/business-digital-communication/

IULM University – Milan - Contract Professor and chair of the course in Corporate Communication and Digital Languages (2007 to 2010) Taught the course "Corporate Communication and Digital Languages" in the Communication, PR and Advertising Faculty.
http://web.archive.org/web/20120225200444/http://www.iulm.it/wps/wcm/connect/iulmit/iulm-it/personale-docenti/istituto-comunicazione-comportamento-e-consumi/docenti-a-contratto/camisani-calzolari-marco

UNIVERSITY OF MILAN (Università Statale di Milano) - Contract Professor in Digital Marketing and Communication (for courses and masters) (2012)

- Taught the course on "Marketing dei progetti innovativi" inside the main course on "Sistemi per la progettazione assistita da calcolatore"; Master IDTV and "Interactive Digital Communication";

BRUNEL UNIVERSITY - London - Lecturer (2012)
Lecturer in Digital Communication

LCA Business School - London - Lecturer (2012)
Lecturer in Digital Communication

TELEVISION

CANALE 5 - Striscia la Notizia (TV Program - 2017 to now)
From September 2017 he participates every WEEK in the program Striscia la Notizia as expert in digital.
- Video:
http://www.striscialanotizia.mediaset.it/ricerca/risultato.shtml?q=CAM

264

ISANI+CALZOLARI&scope=www.striscialanotizia.mediaset.it&sourc
e=www.striscialanotizia.mediaset.it&sort=

RAI 1 - Pronto Soccorso Digitale (TV Program - 2014 to now)
From October 2014 he participates every Saturday in the program
Uno Mattina as expert in digital.
- Video: http://www.dailymotion.com/f501469386

RTL 102.5 - Spazio Tecnologia (Radio Program - 2012 to now)
He participates every Thursday in the morning news program as
expert in digital (now more than 100 episodes from 2012 to now)
- Videos:
https://www.youtube.com/results?search_query=rtl+102.5+camisani
- Website: http://www.rtl.it/redazione/38/Spazio_Tecnologia/

DIGITALK - Talkshow (TV Program - 2004)
Host at Digitalk, the first Italian talk show on Digital technologies,
broadcast daily at 11pm on SKY channel 817 on the website
www.digitalk.tv and on UMTS TIM mobile phones.
- Videos: Video mix - Videos: All episodes

La7 - Misterweb (TV Program - 2001 to 2002)
From September 2001 to January 2002 he presented the TV
programme "MisterWeb", an entertainment about Internet, funny
videos and digital culture. Broadcast every Saturday at 19.30 on
LA7.
- Video: Video Mix

RADIO CAPITAL (Radio Program - 1996)
Program ADV: Internetworkcity
A radio program about Digital Literacy with Fabio Volo (1996)

BOOK WRITER

THE FAKE NEWS BIBLE
Amazon, (2018)

265

FIRST DIGITAL AID FOR BUSINESSES (Pronto Soccorso Digitale per le Aziende)
Published by Hoepli, (2015) - LINK: HOEPLI book page

THE DIGITAL WORLD (Il Mondo Digitale)
Published by Mondadori, (2013) - LINK: Amazon book page

ESCAPE FROM FACEBOOK
CreateSpace, (2012) - LINK: Amazon book page

ENTERPRISE 4.0 - (Impresa 4.0)
Published by Pearson / Financial Times, (2008) - LINK: Amazon book page

KEYNOTE SPEAKER

BUSINESS ROCKS - event with STEVE WOZNIAK; CARTASI (leader company in electronic payments in Italy); ABI (Associazione Bancaria Italiana); SIEMENS (Keynote speaker); The European House AMBROSETTI "Il mondo sulla punta delle dita: la digitalizzazione del marketing e dei media, HEWLETT PACKARD, MICROSOFT, VMWARE; ORACLE "Movement Event" Bologna CNR, RFID and Mobility Solutions; Futurshow; SYMANTEC: Security Black Market"; BOCCONI UNIVERSITY Lecture at JEWC workshop "Innovation in Communication"; UNIVERSITY OF MILAN; INTESA SANPAOLO FORMAZIONE; POLITECNICO DI MILANO; Ordine Degli Ingegneri Di Torino (Engineers association of Turin); DIGITAL VENICE (9.7.2014) Link; IED (IED Snack) Torino (15.5.2014) Link; FINDOMESTIC Roadshow ; BANCA SELLA; VEGA, Science and Technology Park of Venice; CORRIERE DELLA SERA - Corriere Innovazione; ADVEO annual conference; REALE MUTUA ASSICURAZIONI event - Torino; ASSOCALZATURIFICI - Hotel K West - London; NETCOM E-commerce Forum"; CONFINDUSTRIA VENETO; ASSOLOMBARDA "Web marketing e sicurezza informatica"; "FORUM PA", Fair of Rome (10.5.11) – Video of the event; Teacher at the Ambrosetti workshop "Marketing and 4-Directions Digital Communication", Milan;

DIGITAL PROJECT DESIGNER

IKEA Official catalogue and Business Brochure for iPhone\iPad & Android, MTV italian website (1998-1999), RTL 102.5 iOS App, Greenpeace website http://euvsco2.org/, ATM Milano, the official Milanese Transportation Company System, Infrastructure and Transport Ministry website advisor, Gli Amici di Che Banca!, Radio 105 website, 883 / Max pezzali (music band) website, RADIO MONTECARLO website, Social media casting Donna Moderna Mondadori, MUNICIPALITY OF MILAN for the creation of interactive maps, IULM University WebTV, WebTV for the bank Banca Popolare di Vicenza, TIMBERLAND social platform, Livepetitions.com, an international petition platform, Neri per Caso Website, RADIO CAPITAL website, for Claudio Cecchetto in 1996 he created the world's first virtual currency in a web game (EnergyBank) as part of another product (InternetworkCity), the first Italian web based social Network.

ENTREPRENEUR

MEGASHOUTS Ltd. - London - CEO & founder (2015 to now)
A social media amplifier that allows you to send the recipient a message he cannot ignore thanks to the media mechanisms started by Socialbombing. The recipient will receive the message through more than one channel: social networks, newspapers, TV, radio, online advertising, banners, flyers, sandwich boards and other channels capable of generating media buzz. www.megashouts.org

LIVEPETITIONS Ltd. – London - CEO & founder (2007 to now)
The international signature-gathering platform livepetitions.com, now available in 10 countries around the world, with the UK, Italian and French versions (www.firmiamo.it and www.jesigne.fr) leaders in activism sector with 2 millions of active users. www.livepetitions.org

SPEAKAGE – Milan / London - CEO & founder (2004 to now)
A company that develops white label web platforms such as Social Networks, WebTV, Social Media and Viral systems for major international companies like the mobile official IKEA catalogue, iATM - the iPhone app for Milan public transportation - and successful communities like Livepetitions.com or the Greenpeace website for the Europe vs CO2 campaign. www.speakage.com

AudioRete Srl – Milano - CEO & founder (1999 to 2001)
In 2000, he produced Radio3210.com, Italy's first on-demand radio station with a schedule of brand new formats which could be downloaded on demand, 5 years ahead of podcasts.
Business or sector Digital audio productions

UNOPORTALS S.p.A – Milano - Founder & shareholder (1998 to 1999)
with Ibiz Group s.a. (Luxembourg), he founded UnoPortals S.p.A.
Business or sector Internet - Community – Social Network

QUICKWEDDING Srl – Milano - Founder (1997)
Producer of Matrimonionline, the first website for virtual online marriages - www.matrimonionline.com

VARIOUS

● TWITTER FAKE FOLLOWERS STUDIES
● Analysis of Twitter followers of leading international companies and politicians.
     Quantitative and qualitative studies of behaviours demonstrated by humans
     (users which are presumably real) or by bots (users which are presumably fake).
     Quantified the proportion of computer-generated fans or inactive users following big brands and politicians on Twitter. These groundbreaking studies on fake Twitter followers of companies and politicians which generated

a considerable amount of international press coverage, being extensively reviewed by:
REUTERS (Robots crowd Twitter brand profiles: study) - Link
FINANCIAL TIMES (Twitter bots are boosting brands – survey) - Link
GUARDIAN (Hot or bot? Italian professor casts doubt on politician's Twitter popularity) - Link
DAILY TELEGRAPH (Human or 'bot'? Doubts over Italian comic Beppe Grillo's Twitter followers) - Link
THE ECONOMIST (Beware the tweeting crowds) - Link

- AFFILIATED PRACTITIONER AT CENTRE FOR CULTURE MEDIA & REGULATION (CCMR)
- Brunel University - London
- UKTI – UK TRADE & INVESTMENTS (UK GOVERNMENT DEPARTMENT) - LONDON
- Judge and Mentor
- IPSOA Wolters Kluwer
- Course Designer of a Master in Digital.
- ULTIMA RAZZIA
- TV show with Patrizio Roversi and Susy Blady - Co-author of the TV program
- IL SOLE 24 ORE
- Lecturer for the Master "Marketing and Digital Communication"
- METAMONDO
- He published Metamondo, a song and a music video as a manifesto for digital freedom. (2003)
- Video: https://www.youtube.com/watch?v=QgMOSB5yg_4
- ELETTROSHOW Radio program
- https://www.youtube.com/watch?v=ZAn2c6-dN8E (1998)
- AMBASSADOR OF E-SKILLS FOR JOBS

- the European Commission about digital competence
- MEMBER OF MENSA UK
- (the international association for high-IQ individuals)
- AWARDED IN "EXCELLENCE IN COMMUNICATION"
- In 2000 the Centro Studi Comunicazione Cogno in Rome awarded him the prize
- IL SOLE 24 ORE WWW AWARD.
- The MTV website that he designed won the Il Sole 24 ore WWW award.

VOLUNTARY TEACHING

Inspiring students about
digital and tech

- KENSINGTON ALDRIDGE ACADEMY, W10 6EX
- CITY AND ISLINGTON SIXTH FORM COLLEGE, LONDON EC1V 7LA
- VICTORIA CENTRE , LONDON SW1P 2P
- WESTMINSTER KINGSWAY COLLEGE
- ALL SAINTS CATHOLIC SCHOOL AND TECHNOLOGY COLLEGE, DAGENHAM RM8 1JT
- HOLLAND PARK SCHOOL, LONDON W8 7AF
- KENSINGTON ALDRIDGE ACADEMY, W10 6EX
- ROSEDALE COLLEGE, UB3 2SE
- DAGENHAM PARK COFE SCHOOL, RM10 9QH
- BRENTFORD SCHOOL FOR GIRLS, TW8 0PG

30516905R00154

Printed in Poland
by Amazon Fulfillment
Poland Sp. z o.o., Wrocław